STUDIES IN
EARLY ROMAN LITURGY

III
THE ROMAN EPISTLE-LECTIONARY

BY

WALTER HOWARD FRERE, C.R.
D.D., Litt.D.

WIPF & STOCK · Eugene, Oregon

Wipf and Stock Publishers
199 W 8th Ave, Suite 3
Eugene, OR 97401

Studies in Early Roman Liturgy
III. The Roman Epistle - Lectionary
By Frere, W. H.
ISBN 13: 978-1-61097-171-3
Publication date 1/26/2011
Previously published by Oxford University Press, 1935

INTRODUCTION

IN planning two volumes on the subject of the early Roman Lectionaries of the Mass (vols. ii and iii), it seemed advisable to begin with the Gospel-Capitularies, and to leave the Lectionary of Epistles and the like to be dealt with later. The chief reason for this plan lay in the abundance of evidence available for the Gospels as compared with the scantiness available for the rest. In all investigations of this nature the main task is so to piece together a very insufficient amount of material as to make the best of the little that we know, and to bridge over as best we may the gulfs of ignorance that separate isolated and discontinuous bits of knowledge. Where two similar problems form a pair, the better documented one is likely to be able to help out the worse. And so it has proved; the results of the investigation in vol. ii have been of great service here in vol. iii.

It would not be unnatural to presuppose that these twins would be more alike than in fact they are. The scheme that contains the lessons of the Lectionary is no dull reflection of the scheme that emerges from the study of the Gospel-books. It has peculiarities and interests of its own. In some respects it carries back our knowledge of the development of the lectionary-system to an earlier stage than that shown in the Gospel-books.

In general, of course, the method of the two Capitularies is the same. Passages are allotted as being proper to particular days. Four things claimed to be taken specially into account: (1) the great feasts and fasts of the Christian year, with the seasons belonging to them; (2) the saints to be commemorated; (3) special occasions, especially those connected with Baptism, or Ordinations and the Embertides; (4) the localities in which the services were to be held—for Rome was full of local associations which claimed to have some recognition or allusion in the service.[1]

There remained over the many demands for a lesson where no Biblical passage could be claimed as having any special appropriateness; such demands had to be supplied from the passages that had not so far been allotted.

A chief interest in this Capitulary is that it shows this process of residuary allotment going on at an early stage in the development of the Lectionary. The Gospel-books only exhibit a later stage, when such demands had already for the most part been supplied. But the Lectionary, lagging as usual behind, shows (in Chapter IV)

[1] Cp. vol. ii, pp. 87, 88.

this kind of development taking place, not merely as regards weekdays, but even in the series of Sundays.

In any case, the problem of selection and allotment was bound to be more difficult in the Lectionary than in the Gospel-book. The whole of the Old Testament here lay before the selector together with the whole of the New Testament other than the Gospels. The quarry in this case is ten times as extensive as in the other. Further, the task of selection in itself was more difficult; this was especially the case in dealing with the O.T. in spite of the long tradition that had taught Christian people to illuminate each Testament with the light of the other. The selector has done his work in the full current of that tradition, with more reasonableness than is always to be found in such circumstances, but not without some judicious and successful audacities.

The Lectionary made some exacting demands, the like of which did not occur in the Gospel-books. There are in it some remains surviving of the old system which had prescribed three lessons, one from the O.T. as well as the 'Apostle' and the Gospel. Thus there are to be noted, at the opening of the list, and again in Lent and in Embertides, some days which still demanded three. A demand on a larger scale occurs at the great Vigil of Easter, and again, by a sort of reflection, at Whitsun. This set of vigil-lessons doubtless goes back to the earlier days, and represents one of the first parts of the Lectionary to be stabilized.

Coming to the Commune we find the Lectionary forging in front of the corresponding Gospel-book; and, further, it is possible to watch the gradual overtaking as it develops. Here the selector's extensive use of the Sapiential Books is particularly noteworthy, and he appears with credit.

Lastly, attention may be called to a point of a different kind. A distinctive feature of the investigation of these lectionaries is that it has greatly discredited the 'Comes' and all its works. Pseudo-Jerome has been further revealed in Chapter V. The finger-prints which he left on the Letter to Constantius have not been identified; but at least it has become more clear that he has the credit of having imposed on Alcuin—our Patron.

W. H. F.

CONTENTS

THE LIBER COMITIS	1
I. THE SOURCES	25
II. A COMPARISON OF EARLIER AND STANDARD SERIES	29
III. ALCUIN'S LECTIONARY	40
IV. DEVELOPMENT	48
THE MANUSCRIPTS	67
V. THE 'COMES'	73
VI. THE SANCTORALE OF THE 'COMES'	79
VII. THE GOSPELS OF THE COMES MSS.	82
VIII. THEOTINCHUS	84
IX. COMPOSITE LESSONS	91
INDEXES:	
SOURCES	97
PERSONS, SUBJECTS, AND BIBLIOGRAPHY	97
PLACES	99
ABBREVIATIONS	100
LITURGICAL DAYS	100
SCHEDULE OF LITURGICAL EPISTLES AND LESSONS	103

[LIBER COMITIS]^a
from the Corbie Lectionary at Leningrad

[1.] (Rom. i. 1–6.)
Fr's. Paulus seruus Ihu. Xpi . . . .
. . . . uocati I'hu. X'pi D'ni. n'ri.

[1 *a*.] Item lec. Esaie proph. (Is. lxii. 1–4.)
Haec dicit D'ns.
Propter Sion n'. tacebo . . . . Et uocabitur tibi nomen nouum quod os D'ni. nominauit . . . .
. . . . et terra tua inhabitabitur, quia complacuit D'no in te.

II. Item ad s'cam. Maria'. De nocte. Lect. ep. beat. Paul' ap. ad Titu'. (Tit. ii. 11–15.)
K'me apparuit gratia Saluatoris omnibus hominibus . . . .
. . . . Haec loquere et exhortare. in X'po. I'hu. D'no. n'ro.

[II *a*.] (Is. ix. 2, 6, 7.)
Haec dicit D'ns. Populus gentium qui ambulabat . . . . Amodo usque in sempiternum.

III. Item ad s'cam Anastasiam. Mane prima. (Tit. iii. 4–7.)
K'me. apparuit benignitas . . . .
. . . . secundum spem uite eterne. in X'po. I'hu. D'no. n'ro.

[III *a*.] (Is. lxi. 1–3; lxii. 11, 12.)
Hec dicit D'ns. Sp's. D'ni. super me, eo quod . . . .
. . . . glorificandum:
Ecce d. auditum . . . . et vocabunt eos populus sc's. redempti a D'no D'o. n'ro.

---

^a Additions are shown by brackets—round ones are used for the modern biblical reckoning and other editorial additions; square ones for the elucidation of the original text, at omissions, miswritings, and the like.

Liber Comitis

iiii. Item ad s'cm. Petrum. In die. (Heb. i. 1–12.)
Fr's. Multifarie multisque modis . . . .
. . . . et anni tui non deficient.

[iv *a*.] (Is. lii. 6–10.)
Hec dicit D'ns. Propter hoc sciet populus . . . .
. . . . fines terre salutare D'i. nostri.

v. In n't. sci. Stephani.[a] (Acts vi. 8–10; vii. 54–60.)
In dieb. illis Stephanus plenus gratia . . . . qui loquebatur. Audientes . . . . et filium hominis stantem a dextris uirtutis D'i . . . .
. . . . obdormiuit in D'no. I'hu. X'po.

vi. In nat'l. s'ci. Joh. Euangl'.[a] Lectio libri Sapientie. (Ecclus. xv. 1–6.)
Qui timet D'm. faciet bona . . . .
. . . . hereditauit illum D'ns. D's. noster.

[vi *a*.] (Eph. i. 3–7.)
Fr's. benedictus D's. et pater D'ni. n'ri . . . .
. . . . quae superabundauit in nobis per I'hm. X'pm. D'nm. nostrum.

vii. In nat'l. Innocentum.[a] (Apoc. xiv. 1–5.)
In diebus illis. Vidi supra montem . . . .
. . . . sine macula s'. ante thronum D'i.

viii. In octabas D'ni. (Col. i. 25–8.)
F'rs. audistis dispensationem D'i . . . . nunc autem manifestatum est s'cis. eius . . . . quod est X'ps. in uobis . . . . hominem perfectum; in X'po. I'hu. D'no. n'o.[b]

---

ix.[c] Prima dominica post natale domini. (Gal. iv. 1–7.)
Quanto tempore heres . . . . et heres per deum.

[a] With musical notation.
[b] So far the print follows the manuscript closely: but thenceforward the print gives the contents accurately, but not exactly.
[c] Henceforward a standardized transcript, omitting head-pieces and tail-pieces, and so on.

Liber Comitis   3

x. In uigl. Teophaniae. Nonas Ian. (Rom. iii. 19–26.)
Scimus quoniam quecunque . . . .
. . . . ex fide est Jesu . . . .

xi. In Teoph. domini. viii Idus Ian. (Is. lx. 1–6.)
Surge inluminare . . . . domino adnuntiantes.

xii. Dom. prima post Teoph. (Rom. xii. 1–5.)
Obsecro uos per . . . . alter alterius membra.

xiii. In oct. Teoph. Lectio Esaie Prophetae. (Is. xxv, xxviii, xxxv, xli, lii, xii, &c., *compound text*.)
Domine deus meus honorificabo . . . .
. . . . adnuntiate hec in uniuersa terra dicit d. O.

xiv. Dom. secunda post Teoph. (Rom. xii. 6–16.)
Habentes donationes . . . .
. . . . humilibus consentientes.

xv. Dom. tertia post Teophaniam. (Rom. xii. 16–21.)
Nolite esse prudentes . . . . in bono malum.

xvi. Dom. quarta post Teophaniam. (Rom. xiii. 8–10.)
Nemini quicquam debeatis . . . .
. . . . legis est dilectio.

xvii. In nat. S. Sebastiani. (Heb. xi. 33–9.)
Sancti per fidem . . . . probati inuenti sunt.

xviii. In nat. SS. Agnis et Agathae. *Require in ante de Virginibus* (*i.e.* Qui gloriatur, 2 Cor. x. 17—xi. 2).

xix. In Septuagesima. Ad S. Laurentium. (1 Cor. ix. 24—x. 4.)
Nescitis quod hi . . . .
. . . . petra autem erat Christus.

xx. In Sexagesima. Ad S. Paulum. (2 Cor. xi. 19—xii. 9.)
Libenter enim suffertis . . . . virtus Christi.

xxi. In Quinquagesima. Ad S. Petrum. (1 Cor. xiii. 1–13.)
Si linguis . . . . maior autem his est caritas.

XXII. Feria iv. Ad S. Sabinam. (Joel ii. 12–19.)
  Conuertimini ad me . . . .
  . . . . in gentibus. d. d. O.

XXIII. Feria v. Ad S. Georgium. (Is. xxxviii. 1–6.)
  Egrotauit Ezechias . . . . protegam . . . .

XXIV. Feria vi. Ad SS. Johannem et Paulum. (Is. lviii. 1–9.)
  Clama ne cesses . . . .
  . . . . Ecce adsum Quia misericors sum d. D. tuus.

XXV. Feria vii. (Is. lviii. 9–14.)
  Si abstuleritis . . . . locutum est haec.

XXVI. In Quadragesima. Statio ad Lateranos. (2 Cor. vi. 1–10.)
  [H]ortamur uos . . . . et omnia possidentes.

XXVII. Fe. ii. Ad Vincula. (Ezech. xxxiv. 11–16.)
  Ecce ego ipse . . . . et iustitia . . . .

XXVIII. Fe. iii. Ad S. Anastasiam. (Is. lv. 6–11.)
  In diebus. . . .Loquutus est . . . . Quaerite d. . . . .
  . . . . atque misi illud . . . .

XXIX. Fe. iv. Ad S. Mariam. MENSIS PRIMI. (Exod. xxiv. 12–18.)
  In diebus . . . . Dixit d. ad Moysen Ascende . . . . quadraginta noctibus.

[XXIX a.] Item ubi supra. (3 Reg. xix. 3–8.)
  Venit Helias . . . . ad montem dei Horeb.

XXX. Fe. v. Ad S. Laurentium ad Formonsum. (Ezech. xviii. 1–9.)
  Factus est sermo . . . .
  . . . . vita viuet ait d. D.

XXXI. Fe. vi. Ad Apostolos. (Ezech. xviii. 20–8.)
  Anima que peccauerit . . . .
  . . . . non morietur . . . .

Liber Comitis 5

XXXII. Sabbato. Ad S. Petrum in xii lect.
    (*a*) (Deut. xxvi. 15–19.)
        .... Respice d. de .... locutus est tibi.
    (*b*) (Deut. xi. 22–5.)
        .... Si custodieritis ....
        .... calcaturi estis sicut locutus est uobis d. D. v.
    (*c*) (2 Mach. i. 23, 2–5.)
        Orationem faciebant ....
            .... in tempore malo ....
    (*d*) Lectio libri Sap. (Ecclus. xxxvi. 1–10.)
        Miserere nostri .... mirabilia tua ....
    (*e*) (Dan. iii. 49–55, &c., *a liturgical text.*)
        Angelus domini descendebat ....
            .... in saecula.
    (*f*) (1 Thess. v. 14–23.)
        Rogamus uos Corripite ....
        .... sine querela in aduentu d. n. Jesu Christi seruetur.

XXXIII. Dom. prima mensis primi. (1 Thess. iv. 1–7.)
    Rogamus uos et obsecramus ....
        .... sed in sanctificationem ....

XXXIV. Fe. ii. Ad S. Clementem. (Dan. ix. 15–19.)
    Orauit Danihel dicens, Domine D. n. ....
        .... super populum tuum ....

XXXV. Fe. iii. Ad S. Balbinam. (3 Reg. xvii. 8–16.)
    Factus est sermo .... in manu Heliae.

XXXVI. Fe. iv. Ad S. Ceciliam. (Esth. xiii. 9–11; 15–17.)
    Orauit Hester ad d. dicens, Domine deus rex omnipotens .... canentium te ....

XXXVII. Fe. v. Ad S. Laurentium.[a] (Jer. xvii. 5–10.)
    .... Maledictus homo ....
        .... adinuentionum suarum ....

    [a] In the Capitula, 'Ad S. Mariam trans Tiberim'; and rightly so.

XXXVIII. Fe. vi. Ad S. Uitalem. (Gen. xxxvii. 6–22.)
.... Audite somnium ....
       .... reddere patri suo.

XXXIX. Sabb. Ad SS. Marcellinum et Petrum. (Gen. xxvii. 6–39.)
Dixit Rebecca filio .... Audiui patrem ....
       .... benedictio tua.

XL. Dom. in XXX. Ad S. Laurentium. Ebd. iii. (Eph. v. 1–9.)
Estote imitatores .... et veritate.

XLI. Feria ii. Ad S. Marcum. (4 Reg. v. 1–15.)
Naaman princeps ....
       .... nisi tantum d. D. Israel.

XLII. Feria iii. Ad S. Potentianam. (4 Reg. iv. 1–7.)
Mulier quedam clamabat ....
       .... viuite de reliquo.

XLIII. Feria iv. Ad S. Syxtum. (Exod. xx. 12–24.)
Honora patrem ....
       .... fuerit nominis mei.

XLIV. Feria v. Ad SS. Cosmam et Damianum. (Jer. vii. 1–7; xlii. 12.)
Factum est uerbum .... [Sta in porta] ....
       .... usque in saeculum ....

XLV. Feria vi. Ad S. Laurentium. (Num. xx. 2, 3, 6–13.)
Conuenerunt filii Israhel ....
       .... sanctificatus est in eis.

XLVI. Sabbato. Ad S. Susannam. (Dan. xiii. parts of 1–62.)
Erat vir in Babylone ....
       .... est innoxius in die illa.

[XLVII.]^a Dom. XX. [ad hierusalem.]^a (Gal. iv. 22—v. 1.)
Scriptum est enim ....
       .... Christus nos liberauit.

^a Omitted in the Capitula.

Liber Comitis 7

XLVIII. Feria ii. Ad SS. Quatuor Coronatos. (3 Reg. iii. 16–28.)
 Venerunt due mulieres . . . .
    . . . . ad faciendum iudicium.

XLIX. Feria iii. Ad S. Laurentium in Damasi. (Exod. xxxii. 7–14.)
 Loquutus . . . . Discende de monte . . . .
    . . . . misertus est populo suo.

L. Feria iv. Ad S. Paulum in Mediana. (Ezech. xxxvi. 23–8.)
 Sanctificabo nomen . . . .
    . . . . ero uobis in deum . . . .

[L a.] Item ubi supra. (Is. i. 16–19.)
 Lauamini, mundi estote . . . .
    . . . . terre comedetis . . . .

LI. Feria v. Ad [S. Silvestrum].ᵃ (4 Reg. iv. 25–38.)
 Venit mulier serupthis . . . .
    . . . . reuersus est in galgala.

LII. Feria vi. Ad S. Eusebium. (3 Reg. xvii. 17–24.)
 Egrotauit filius . . . . in tuo ore verum est.

LIII. Sabbato. Ad S. Laurentium in media aurium apertionum. (Is. xlix. 8–15.)
 Tempore placito . . . . non obliviscar tui . . . .

[LIII a.] Item ut supra. (Is. lv. 1–11.)
 Omnes sitientes venite . . . . de ore meo . . . .

LIV. Dom. quinta. Ad S. Petrum in XVma.ᵇ (Heb. ix. 11–15.)
 Christus adsistens . . . .
    . . . . aeterne hereditatis . . . .

LV. Feria ii. Ad S. Crisogonum. (Jonas iii. 1–10.)
 Factum est verbum . . . .
    . . . . populo suo d. D. n.

ᵃ The manuscript has ad SS. Cosmam et Damianum: a mistake that must have come in at the insertion of the Lenten Thursdays.
ᵇ The Station is omitted in the Capitula.

Liber Comitis

LVI. Feria iii. Ad S. Quiriacum. (Dan. xiv. 28–42.)
Congregati sunt Babylonii . . . .
. . . . de lacu leonum.

LVII. Feria iv. Ad S. Marcellum. (Lev. xix. 1, 2, 10–19.)
Locutus est d. . . . . Ego d. D. v. . . . .
. . . . Ego enim sum d. vester.

LVIII. Feria v. Ad S. Apollinarem. (Dan. iii. 35–45.)
Orauit Danihel dicens . . . .   d. D. ne despicias populum t. . . . .   super omnem terram . . . .

LIX. Feria vi. Ad S. [Stephanum]ᵃ. (Jer. xvii. 13–18.)
Dixit Jeremias, Domine, omnes qui te . . . .
. . . . contere eos . . . .

LX. Sabbato. (Jer. xviii. 18–23.)
Dixerunt impii . . . . furoris tui . . . .

LXI. Dom. indulgentia. Ad Lateranis. (Phil. ii. 5–11.)
Hoc sentite . . . . dei patris.

LXII. Feria ii. Ad SS. Nereum et Achilleum. (Is. l. 5–10.)
Dixit Esaias, Dominus D. aperuit . . . .
. . . . innitatur super d. D. suo.

[LXII a.] Item ubi supra. (Zach. xi. 12—xiii. 9.)
Si bonum est . . . . et ipse dicet d. D. t.

LXIII. Feria iii. Ad S. Priscam. (Jer. xi. 18–20.)
Dixit Jeremias, Domine demonstrasti . . . .
. . . . causam meam . . . .

[LXIII a.] Item ubi supra. (Sap. ii. 12–22.)
Dixerunt impii Iudei apud semet ipsos, Venite circumueniamus . . . .
. . . . animarum suarum.

LXIV. Feria iv. Ad S. Mariam. (Is. lxii. 11; lxiii. 1, 5, 7.)
Dicite filie Sion, Ecce saluator . . . . cum eo.
Quis est iste . . . . que reddidit nobis d. D. n.

ᵃ The manuscript repeats Apollinaris by mistake: the Capitula gives no Station.

Liber Comitis 9

[LXIV a.] Ut supra. (Is. liii. 1–12.)
  Domine quis credidit....
     .... ut non perirent....

LXV. Feria v. Quando crisma conficitur. (1 Cor. xi. 20–32.)
  Conuenientibus ergo uobis....
     .... cum hoc mundo damnemur.

LXVI. Feria vi. Ad Hierusalem. (Hosea vi. 1–6.)
  In tribulatione sua....
     .... plus quam holocausta.

[LXVI a.] Item ubi supra. (Exod. xii. 1–11.)
  Dixit d. ad Moysen et Aaron....
     .... transitus domini.
  Explicit de Quadragesima.

[LXVI*.] INCIPIUNT LECTIONES DE PASCHA.
 (*a*) Lectio libri Genesis (i. 1—ii. 2).
  In principio creauit.... .... patrarat.
 (*b*) Item II. (Gen. v. 31—viii. 21, *compound*.)
  Noe vero cum.... .... odorem suauitatis.
 (*c*) Item III. (Genesis xxii. 1–19.)
  Temptauit deus Abraham....
     .... habitauit ibi.
 (*d*) Item IV. (Exod. xiv. 24—xv. 1.)
  Factum est in uigilia.... .... et dixerunt.
 (*e*) Item EIUSMODI CARMEN.
  Cantemus domino gloriose....
     .... nomen est illi.
 (*f*) Item v. (Is. liv. 17—lv. 11.)
  Haec est hereditas.... .... de ore meo....
 (*g*) Item vi. (Baruch iii. 9–38.)
  Audi Israel mandata.... (*compound*)
     .... conuersatus est.
 (*h*) Item ut supra VII. (Ezech. xxxvii. 1–14.)
  Et facta est super me.... .... uos faciam....

Liber Comitis

(*j*) VIII. Lectio Isaie prophetae (iv. 1–6).
    Apprehendent .... et a pluuia. *with*

(*k*)   CANTICUM (v. 1, 2, 7).
    Vinea facta est ....
            .... domus Israhel est.

(*l*) IX. (Exod. xii. 1–11.)
    Dixit d. ad Moysen .... Mensis iste ....
            .... transitus domini.

(*m*) X. (Jonas iii. 1–10.)
    Factum est uerbum .... surge uade ....
            .... misertus est populo suo ....

(*n*) XI. (Deut. xxxi. 22–30.)
    Scripsit Moyses canticum .... compleuit. *with*

(*o*)   CANTICUM. (Deut. xxxii. 1–4.)
    Adtende caelum et loquar .... iustus et sanctus d.

(*p*) XII. (Dan. iii. 1–24.)
    Nabuchodonosor rex fecit statuam .... benedicentes dominum. *with*

(*q*)   CANTICUM in Ps. xl. (1–3).
    Sicut ceruus desiderat .... ubi est deus tuus.

LXVII. Sabbato sancto. Ad Lateranis. (Col. iii. 1–4.)
    Si consurrexistis .... cum ipso in gloria.

LXVIII. Dominica. Ad S. Mariam. (1 Cor. v. 7, 8.)
    Expurgate vetus .... et veritatis.

LXIX. Feria ii. Ad S. Petrum. (Acts x. 37–43.)
    Stans Petrus .... credunt in eum.

LXX. Feria iii. Ad S. Paulum. (Acts xiii. 16, 26–33.)
    Surgens Paulus .... resuscitans Jesum ....

LXXI. Feria iv. Ad S. Laurentium. (Acts x. 34; iii. 12–19.)
    Aperiens Petrus os .... vestra peccata.

Liber Comitis

LXXII. Feria v. Ad Apostolos. (Acts viii. 26–40.)
   Angelus domini locutus . . . .
                   . . . . predicans nomen d. J. C.

LXXIII. Feria vi. Ad S. Mariam. (1 Pet. iii. 18–22.)
   Christus semel . . . . in dextera dei.

LXXIV. Feria vii. Ad Lateranis. (1 Pet. ii. 1–10.)
   Deponentes omnem . . . .
                   . . . . misericordiam consecuti.

LXXV. Dom. Octau. Paschae. (1 Jo. v. 4–10.)
   Omne quod natum . . . . dei in se.

LXXVI. Prima dom. post Pasche. (1 Pet. ii. 21–5.)
   Christus passus est . . . .
                   . . . . animarum vestrarum.

LXXVII. Secunda dom. post Pasche. (1 Pet. ii. 11–20.)
   Obsecro tanquam . . . . gratia in C. J. d. n.

LXXVIII. In Ntl. SS. Apost. Philippi et Jacobi. (Sap. v. 1–5.)
   Stabunt iusti in . . . . sors illorum est.

LXXIX. Tertia dom. post Oct. Pasche. (Jas. i. 17–21.)
   Omne datum . . . . animas vestras.

LXXX. V NON. MAII. Inuentio S. Crucis. (Gal. v. 10—vi. 14.)
   Confido in uobis . . . . et ego mundo.

LXXXI. Quarta dom. post Oct. Pasche. (Jas. i. 22–7.)
   Estote factores . . . . ab hoc seculo.

LXXXII. In Letania maiore. (Jas. v. 16–20.)
   Confitemini alterutrum . . . . peccatorum.

LXXXIII. In vig. Ascensa domini. (Acts iv. 32–5.)
   Multitudinis autem . . . . opus erat.

LXXXIV. In Ascensa domini. (Acts i. 1–11.)
   Primum quidem sermonem . . . .
                   . . . . in caelum.

Liber Comitis

LXXXV. Dom. post Ascensa domini. (1 Pet. iv. 8–11.)
Estote prudentes ....
.... honorificetur deus per J. C. d. n.

LXXXVI. In Sabbato Pentecostes.
(*a*) In Genesi. In principio fecit Deus caelum. I.
(*b*) De Abraham. Temptauit deus Abraham. II.
(*c*) In Exodo. Factum est in uig. mat. *cum cantic.* III.
(*d*) In Deuteron. Scripsit Moyses. *cum cantic.* IV.
(*e*) In Isaia. Apprehendent. *cum cantic.* Vinea domini. V.
(*f*) In Hieremia. Audi Israel mandata. VI.
(*g*) De psalmo xl. Sicut ceruus.
et legis lect.
(*h*) (Acts xix. 1–8.)
Cum Apollo esset .... de regno dei.

LXXXVII. In Dom. Pentecostes. (Acts ii. 1–11.)
Cum complerentur .... magnalia dei.

LXXXVIII. Feria ii. Ad Vincula. (Acts x. 34, 42–8.)
Aperiens Petrus os .... nobis precipit ....
.... in nomine D. J. C.

LXXXIX. Feria iii. Ad S. Anastasiam. (Acts viii. 14–16.)
Cum audissent apostoli ....
.... spiritum sanctum.

XC. Feria iv. Ad S. Mariam. (Acts ii. 14–21.)
Stans Petrus .... saluus erit.

[XC *a*.] Item ut supra. (Acts v. 12–16.)
Per manus Apostolorum ....
.... curabantur omnes.

XCI. Feria v. Ad Apostolos. (Acts viii. 5–8.)
Philippus descendens .... in illa ciuitate.

XCII. Feria vi. Ad SS. Johannem et Paulum. (Acts ii. 22–28.)
Aperiens Petrus .... Viri Israhelite ....
.... cum facie tua.

Liber Comitis 13

xciii. Sabbato. Ad S. Stephanum. (Acts xiii. 44–52.)
  Conuenit uniuersa . . . .
            . . . . gaudio et spiritu sancto.

xciv. Dom. Octauas Pentecosten. (Apoc. iv. 1–9.)
  Vidi ostium apertum . . . .   viuentem in saec. s.

[xciv *a*.] Item. (Acts v. 29–42.)
  Respiciens autem Petrus . . . .
            . . . . euangelizantes Jesum Christum.

xcv. Ebd. secunda post Pent. (1 Jo. iv. 16–21.)
  Deus caritas est . . . . fratrem suum.

xcvi. Ebd. iii. post Pent. (1 Jo. iii. 13–18.)
  Nolite mirari . . . . opere et veritate.

INCIPIUNT LECTIONES MENSIS QUARTI.

xcvii. Feria iv. Ad S. Mariam. (Sap. i. 1–7.)
  Dixit Salomon filiis Israhel, Diligite iustitiam . . . .
            . . . . scientiam habet vocis.

[xcvii *a*.] (Is. xliv. 1–3.)
  Audi Iacob . . . . generationem tuam . . . .

xcviii. Feria vi. Ad Apostolos. (Joel ii. 23, 24, 26, 27.)
  Exultate filii Sion . . . . meus in eternum . . . .

[xcviii*.]   Sabbato.[a] Ad S. Petrum.
  (*a*) (Joel ii. 28–32.)
     . . . . Effundam de spiritu meo . . . . saluus erit.
  (*b*) Item ubi supra. (Lev. xxiii. 9–11, 15–17, 20, 21.)
     Dixit . . . . Loquere filiis . . . .
            . . . . generationibus vestris . . . .
  (*c*) Item ut supra. (Deut. xxvi. 1–3, 7–11.)
     Dixit Moyses Audi Israel . . . .
            . . . . dederit tibi.
  (*d*) Item ut supra. (Lev. xxvi. 3–12.)
     Dixit . . . . Si in preceptis . . . .
            . . . . populus meus . . . .

[a] Sabbato has no number in the Comes, and is omitted in the Capitula.

(e) Hic legitur Danihel propheta . . . .
. . . . *Require mens. prim.*

(f) (Rom. v. 1–5.)
Justificati igitur . . . . datus est nobis.

xcix. Ebd. iv post Pent. (1 Pet. v. 6–11.)
Humiliamini sub potente . . . .
. . . . in saecula saeculorum.

c. Ebd. v post Pent. (Rom. viii. 18–23.)
Existimo enim quod . . . .
. . . . redemptionem corporis nostri . . . .

ci. In vig. S. Johannis Bapt. . . . . . VIII KAL. JUL. (Jer. i. 4–10.)
Factum est verbum . . . . et plantes.

cii. In die nat. S. Johannis Baptistae. (Is. xlix. 1–3, 5, 6, 7.)
Audite insule . . . . qui elegit te.

ciii. Ebd. vi post Pent. (1 Pet. iii. 8–15.)
Omnes unanimes . . . .
. . . . in cordibus uestris.

civ. In vigilia S. Petri. III KAL. JUL. (Acts iii. 1–10.)
Petrus et Johannes . . . .
. . . . quod contigerat illi.

cv. In nat. S. Petri. (Acts xii. 1–11.)
Misit Herodes rex . . . . plebis Iudeorum.

cvi. In vigilia S. Pauli Apostoli. (Gal. i. 11–24.)
Notum vobis facio . . . .
. . . . in me clarificabant d. J. C.

cvii. In nat. S. Pauli. PRID. KAL. JUL. (Acts ix. 1–23.)
Saulus adhuc spirans . . . .
. . . . quoniam hic est Christus.

Liber Comitis 15

cviii. Ebd. vii post Pent. (Rom. vi. 3–11.)
Quicunque baptizati ....
.... viuentes autem deo in C. J. d. n.

cix. In oct. Apostolorum. (Ecclus. xliv. 10–15.)
Hi sunt viri misericordie ....
.... ecclesia sanctorum.

cx. Ebd. viii post Pent. (Rom. vi. 19–23.)
Humanum dico .... uita eterna in C. J. d. n.

cxi. Ebd. ix post Pent. (Rom. viii. 12–17.)
Debitores sumus ....
.... coheredes autem Christi.

cxii. Ebd. x post Pent. (1 Cor. x. 6–13.)
Non simus concupiscentes ....
.... ut possitis sustinere.

— viii kal. aug.[a] Nat. S. Iacobi Apostoli.
Justum deduxit ....
.... *Require in antea de Sanctorum.* (cli *a*.)

cxiii. Ebd. xi post Pent. (1 Cor. xii. 2–11.)
Scitis quoniam cum gentes ....
.... prout vult.

cxiv. kal. aug. Nat. S. Felicitatis. (Prov. xxxi. 10–31.)
Mulierem fortem .... opera eius.

cxv. Ebd. xii post Pent. (1 Cor. xv. 1–10.)
Notum uobis facio .... vacua non fuit.

cxvi. In vig. S. Laurentii. (Ecclus. li. 1–8, 12.)
Confitebor tibi d. Rex ....
.... de manibus angustie d. D. n.

cxvii. In nat. S. Laurentii. (2 Cor. ix. 6–10.)
Qui parce seminat .... iustitie vestre.

[a] The entry is not in the Capitula.

Liber Comitis

[CXVIII.]^a XVII KAL. SEPT. Adsumptio S. Mariae. (Ecclus. xxiv. 11–13, 15–20.)
 In omnibus requiem quesiui . . . .
      . . . . suauitatem odoris.

CXIX. Ebd. xiii post Pent. (2 Cor. iii. 4–9.)
 Fiduciam talem . . . . iustitiae in gloria.

— In nat. S. Bartholomei Apostoli.^c Lectio ad Ephesios (ii. 19–22).
 Jam non estis hospites . . . .
      . . . . ciues sanctorum.

CXX. III^b KAL. SEPT. Passio S. Johannis Baptiste. (Prov. x. 28, 32; xi. 3–6, 8–11.)
 Expectatio iustorum . . . .
      . . . . exaltabitur ciuitas.

CXXI. Ebd. xiv post Pent. (Gal. iii. 16–22.)
 Abrahe dicte sunt . . . . daretur credentibus.

CXXII. Ebd. xv post Pent. (Gal. v. 16–24.)
 Spiritu ambulate . . . . et concupiscentiis.

— VI. ID. SEPT. Natiuitas S. Marie.^c Lectio. In omnibus requiem quesiui. *Require in Adsumptione eius.* (CXVIII.)

CXXIII. Ebd. xvi post Pent. (Gal. v. 25—vi. 10.)
 Si spiritu uiuimus . . . .
      . . . . ad domesticos fidei.

— XVIII. KAL. OCT. Exaltatio S. Crucis.^c (Phil. ii. 5–11.)
Hoc sentite in uobis. *Require dom. in Palmis.* (LXI.)

CXXIV. Ebd. xvii post Pent. (Eph. iii. 13–21.)
 Obsecro uos ne deficiatis . . . .
      . . . . saeculi saeculorum. Amen.

---

^a The number is supplied from the Capitula.
^b The Capitula has iv Kal Sept.
^c The entry is not in the Capitula.

Liber Comitis

cxxv. Ebd. xviii post Pent. (Eph. iv. 1–6.)
  Obsecro itaque uos ego vinctus . . . .
    . . . . benedictus in saecula saeculorum.

  INCIPIUNT LECTIONES MENSIS VII.

cxxvi. Feria iv. Ad S. Mariam. (Amos ix. 13–15.)
  Ecce dies ueniunt . . . . dedi eis . . . .

[cxxvi *a*.] (2 Esdr. viii. parts of 1–10.)
  Congregatus est omnis . . . . fortitudo nostra.

cxxvii. Feria vi. Ad Apostolos. (Hosea xiv. 2–10.)
  Conuertere Israhel ad d. Dicite ei . . . .
    . . . . ambulabunt in eis.

cxxviii (*a*) Sabbato. Ad S. Petrum in xii lect. (Lev. xxiii. 27–32.)
  Locutus est . . . . Decimo die . . . .
    . . . . sabbata vestra . . . .

(*b*) Item supra. (Lev. xxiii. 39–43.)
  Loquutus est . . . . Quinto decimo die . . . .
    . . . . Ego d. D. uester.

(*c*) Item supra. (Mich. vii. 14, 16, 18–20.)
  Domine deus noster pasce . . . .
    . . . . diebus antiquis.

(*d*) (Zach. viii. 1, 2, 14–19.)
  Factum est verbum . . . .
    . . . . pacem diligite dicit d. exercituum.

(*e*) *Hic legitur Daniel.*

(*f*) Item ubi supra. (Heb. ix. 2–12.)
  Tabernaculum factum est . . . . inuenta.

cxxix. Ebd. xviiii post Pent. (1 Cor. i. 4–8.)
  Gratias ago . . . . in die aduentus d. n. J. C.

— XII KAL. OCT. Vig. S. Matthaei.[a] (Prov. iii. 13–20.)
  Beatus uir qui inuenit sapientiam . . . .
    . . . . nubes rore concrescunt.

[a] The entry is not in the Capitula.

— XI KAL. OCT. Nat. S. Matthaei Apostoli.[a] (Eph. iv. 7.)
Unicuique nostrum data . . . . est gratia.

CXXX. In nat. S. Angeli Michahelis. III KAL. OCT. (Apoc. i. 1–5.)
Significauit deus . . . . in sanguine suo.

CXXXI. Ebd. xx post Pent. (Eph. iv. 23–8.)
Renouamini spiritu . . . . patienti.

CXXXII. Ebd. xxi post Pent. (Eph. v. 15–21.)
Videte itaque . . . . in timore Christi.

CXXXIII. Ebd. xxii post Pent. (Eph. vi. 10–17.)
De cetero confortamini in d. . . . .
    . . . . uerbum dei.

CXXXIV. Ebd. xxiii post Pent. (Phil. i. 6–11.)
Confidimus in d. . . . . laudem dei.

CXXXV. Ebd. xxiv post Pent. (Phil. iii. 17—iv. 3.)
Imitatores mei . . . . in libro vitae.

— VI KAL. NOV. Vig. Apostolorum Simonis et Iude.[a] (Sap. iii. 1–8.) Justorum anime . . . .

— In nat. Simonis et Iude.[a] (Rom. viii. 28.)
Scimus enim quoniam . . . .

CXXXVI. Ebd. xxv post Pent. (Col. i. 9–11.)
Non cessamus . . . . cum gaudio . . .

CXXXVII. In vig. S. Andree Apostoli. III KAL. DEC. (Prov. x. 6; Ecclus. xliv. 26, 27; xlv. 2–4, 6–9.)
Benedictio domini . . . . corona gloriae.

CXXXVIII. In nat. S. Andree Apostoli. PRID. KAL. DEC. (Rom. x. 10–18.)
Corde enim creditur . . . . verba eorum.

[a] The entry is not in the Capitula.

Liber Comitis

INCIPIUNT LECTIONES DE ADUENTU DOMINI.

CXXXIX. Ebd. v ante nat. domini. (Jer. xxiii. 5–8.)
Ecce dies venient . . . . et suscitabo . . . .
. . . . in terra sua . . . .

CXL. Ebd. iv ante nat. domini. (Rom. xiii. 11–14.)
Scientes tempus quia . . . .
. . . . induimini d. J. C.

CXLI. Ebd. iii ante nat. domini. (Rom. xv. 4–13.)
Quecumque scripta . . . . spiritus sancti.

CXLII. Ebd. ii ante nat. domini. (1 Cor. iv. 1–5.)
Sic nos existimet . . . . unicuique a deo.

INCIPIUNT LECTIONES MENSIS DECIMI.

CXLIII. Feria iv. Ad S. Mariam. (Is. ii. 1–5.)
. . . . Erit in nouissimis . . . .
. . . . in lumine d. D. nostri.

[CXLIII a.] Ubi supra. (Is. vii. 10–15.)
Loquutus est d. ad Achaz . . . .
. . . . eligere bonum.

CXLIV. Feria vi. Ad Apostolos. (Is. xi. 1–5.)
Egredietur uirga . . . . renum eius.

CXLV. (a) Sabbato. Ad S. Petrum in xii lect. (Is. xix. 20–22.)
Clamabunt ad d. . . . . sanabit eos d. D. n.
(b) Item. (Is. xxxv. 1–7.)
Letabitur deserta . . . .
. . . . in fontes aquarum . . . .
(c) Item. (Is. xl. 9–11.)
Super montem excelsum . . . .
. . . . leuabit eos d. D. n.
(d) Item. (Is. xlv. 1–8.)
Hec dicit d. christo meo . . . .
. . . . ego d. creaui eum.
(e) *Legitur Danihel propheta.*
(f) (2 Thess. ii. 1–8.)
Rogamus uos per . . . . aduentus sui.

CXLVI. Ebdomada prima ante nat. domini. (Phil. iv. 4–7.)
Gaudete in d. . . . . intelligentias uestras . . . .

CXLVII. (*a*) In uig. Omnium Apostolorum. (Prov. iii. 13–20.)
Beatus homo qui inuenit sapientiam . . . .
. . . . concrescunt.
(*b*) (Ecclus. xxxi. 8–11.)
Beatus vir qui inuentus [est sine] . . . .
. . . . omnis ecclesia sanctorum.

CXLVIII. (*a*) In nat. Apostolorum. (Eph. ii. 19–22.)
Jam non estis . . . . dei in spiritu sancto.
(*b*) Item ubi supra. (Eph. iv. 7–13.)
Unicuique nostrum . . . .
. . . . plenitudinis christi d. n.
(*c*) [Item.] (Rom. viii. 28–39.)
Scimus quoniam diligentibus . . . .
. . . . caritate dei quae est in C. J. d. n.

CXLIX. In uig. unius Sacerdotis. (2 Tim. iv. 1–8.)
Testificor coram D. . . . . aduentum eius.

CL.[a] (*a*) In nat. unde supra. (Ecclus. xliv. 16, 17, 20, 22, 25–7; xlv. 3, 8, 19, 20.)
Ecce sacerdos magnus . . . .
. . . . in odorem suauitatis.
(*b*) [Item.] (Heb. vii. 23–7.)
Plures facti sunt . . . . offerendo.
(*c*) Item. (Heb. xiii. 9–16.)
Doctrinis variis . . . . promeretur D.

CLI. (*a*) In uig. unius Confessoris siue martyris. (Ecclus. xxxix. 6–13.)
Iustus cor suum tradidit . . . .
. . . . in generationem.
(*b*) Item in nat. unde supra. (Ecclus. xiv. 22; xv. 3, 4, 6.)
Beatus vir qui in sapientia . . . .
. . . . hereditabit illum . . . .

---

[a] The numbers from CL–CLX are given incorrectly in the manuscript as CLX–CLXX; here therefore the numbers thenceforward are not given as in the Comes, but as they are correctly given in the Capitula prefixed to the Comes.

Liber Comitis 21

(*c*) Item ubi supra. (Sap. iv. 7–11, 13–15.)
   Iustus autem si morte . . . . in electos illius.

(*d*) Item. (Sap. x. 10–14.)
   Iustum deduxit d. . . . .
                        . . . . claritatem aeternam . . . .

(*e*) [Item.] (2 Cor. i. 3–7.)
   Benedictus D. et pater . . . .
                        . . . . et consolationis . . . .

(*f*) [Item.] (2 Tim. ii. 8–10; iii. 10–12.)
   Memor esto . . . . patiuntur.

(*g*) [Item.] (1 Cor. iv. 9–14.)
   Spectaculum facti . . . . moneo . . . .

(*h*) [Item.] (2 Thess. i. 3–10.)
   Gratias agere debemus . . . . crediderunt . . . .

CLII. (*a*) In nat. plurimorum Sanctorum. (Prov. xv. 2–4; 6–9.)
   Lingua sapientium . . . . diligitur a domino.

(*b*) [Item.] (Sap. v. 16–20, 22.)
   Iusti in perpetuo . . . . deducet illos d. D. n.

(*c*) [Item.] (1 Pet. i. 3–7.)
   Benedictus D. et pater . . . . igne probatur.

(*d*) [Item.] (1 Pet. iv. 1–11.)
   Christo igitur passo . . . .
                        . . . . imperium in saecula saeculorum.

CLIII. (*a*) In nat. plurimorum Martyrum. (Sap. iii. 1–8.)
   Iustorum anime in manu . . . .
                        . . . . in perpetuum.

(*b*) Item ut supra. (Prov. x. 28–32; xi. 3–6, 8–11.)
   Expectatio iustorum . . . .
                        . . . . exaltabitur ciuitas.

(*c*) [Item.] (Sap. x. 17–21.)
   Reddet deus mercedem . . . .
                        . . . . laudauerunt pariter . . . .

(*d*) [Item.] (Heb. x. 32–8.)
   Rememoramini . . . . ex fide viuit.

(*e*) Item. (Heb. xi. 33–9.)
   Sancti per fidem . . . . inuenti sunt.

Liber Comitis

CLIV. (*a*) In nat. Uirginum. (Ecclus. li. 1–8, 12.)
    Confitebor tibi d. rex . . . .
            . . . . de manu gentium . . .
    (*b*) [Item.] (Ecclus. li. 13–17.)
    Domine D. meus exaltasti . . . .
            . . . . benedicam nomini tuo . . .
    (*c*) [Item.] Ecclus. xxiv. 1–5; 21, 22.)
    Sapientia laudabit . . . . honores et gloriae.
    (*d*) [Item.] (Sap. vii. 30; viii. 1–4.)
    Sapientia vincit . . . . disciplina dei.

CLV. In ordinatione diaconorum. (1 Tim. iii. 8–13.)
    Diaconos constitue pudicos . . . .
            . . . . fidei quae est in C. J. d. n.

CLVI. In ordinatione presbiterorum. (Tit. i. 1–9.)
    Paulus seruus dei . . . . doctrina sana . . .

CLVII. (*a*) In ordinatione Episcoporum. (Tit. i. 7–9; 1 Tim. ii. 3.)
    Oportet episcopum . . . .
            . . . . acceptum coram D. salvatore nostro.
    (*b*) Item ubi supra. (1 Tim. iii. 1–7; Tit. ii. 10.)
    Fidelis sermo . . . .
            . . . . ut doctrinam dei n. ornet in omnibus.

CLVIII. (*a*) In ieiunio de nat. Pape. (Tobitas xiii. 12–19.)
    . . . . Benedicens Tobias filio suo ait, reedificet d. D. temporibus tuis tabernaculum . . . .
            . . . . a cunctis tribulationibus eius . . .
    (*b*) Item ubi supra. (Deut. xxvii. 14; xxviii. 1–10.)
    Pronuntiabunt Leuite . . . . faciat te d. D. tuus excelsiorem . . . . inuocatum sit super te.
    (*c*) Item ubi supra. (Heb. v. 1–6.)
    Omnis pontifex . . . . Melchisedech.

CLIX. (*a*) In dedicatione Ecclesiae. (Apoc. xxi. 2–5.)
    Uidi ciuitatem . . . . facio omnia.
    (*b*) (1 Cor. iii. 8–15.)
    Unusquisque propriam . . . . per ignem.

Liber Comitis

CLX. In dedicatione oratorii. (Apoc. xxi. 9–27.)
Uenit angelus et locutus ....
.... Ueni ostendam .... in libro uite et agni.

CLXI. (*a*) In aduentu episcopi. (2 Reg. vii. 8–17.)
Ego tuli te .... verba haec.
(*b*) Item. (Acts xx. 17–35.)
Cum venisset Paulus .... quam accipere.
(*c*) Item ut supra. (2 Tim. ii. 22—iii. 7.)
Iuuenilia desideria .... veritatis peruenientes.

[CLXII.] Ad sponsam benedicendum. (1 Cor. vi. 15–20.)
Nescitis quoniam corpora ....
.... in corpore vestro.

[CLXIII.] In Benedictione vidue que fuerit castitatem professa. (1 Cor. vii. 39, 40.)
Mulier iuncta est .... spiritum dei habeo ....

[CLXIV.] (*a*) In Letania tempore belli. (4 Reg. xix *or* Is. xxxvii. 1–7.)
Cum audisset rex Ezechias verba ....
.... [in terra sua. Quia] ego sum d. D. faciens mirabilia.
(*b*) Item ubi supra. (Is. xxxvii. 15–17; 20–35.)
Orauit Ezechias ....
Domine exercituum .... seruum meum ....
(*c*) Item ubi supra. (Jer. viii. 4; Is. xl. 8.)
Numquid qui cadit non resurget? Et qui auersus est non reuertetur? Quia verbum domini manet in eternum et in saec. seculi.

[CLXV.] (*a*) In die belli. (Jer. xlii. 7–12.)
Factum ....
.... vocauit Iohanan .... in terra vestra.
(*b*) Item. (Thren. iii. 22, 24–6, 31, 32, 40, 41, 56, 57.)
Loquutus est .... Misericordie domini quia non sumus consumpti .... dixisti Ne timeas, quia ego sum d. D. t.

Liber Comitis

[CLXVI.] In sterilitate pluuiae. (Jer. xiv. 19–22.)
  Numquid proiciens . . . .
        . . . . fecisti omnia haec.

[CLXVII.] Item ubi supra. (Jer. xvii. 5–10.)
  Maledictus homo . . . .
      . . . . adinuentionum suarum . . . .

[CLXVIII.] Pro ubertate pluuie. (Thren. ii. 19, 20; iii. 53–8.)
  Loquutus est . . . . Consurge, lauda . . . .
      . . . . redemptor vite mee . . . .

[CLXIX.] In aduentu iudicum. (1 Tim. ii. 1–7.)
  Obsecro vos primum . . . . et veritate.

[CLXX.] Contra iudices male agentes. (Is. v. 8–26.)
  Vae qui coniungitis . . . .
      . . . . manus eius extenta.

[CLXXI.] Contra episcopos male agentes. (Ezech. xxxiv. 2–14.)
  Ve pastoribus Israhel . . . .
      . . . . in montibus Israel . . . .

[CLXXII.] (*a*) Ad profi[cis]cendum in itinere. (Gen. xxiv. 7.)
  Loquutus est Abraham dicens, Domine D. caeli . . . .
      . . . . coram te.

 (*b*) Item. (Gen. xlvi. 1–4.)
  Profectusque est Israel . . . .
      . . . . te reuertentem.

[CLXXIII.] Ad missam votiuam. (Is. xviii. 7; xix. 4, 19, 21, 22, 24, 25.)
  In die illa defertur . . . .
      . . . . hereditas mea Israhel . . . .

[CLXXIV.] Pro infirmo. (Jas. v. 13–16.)
  Tristatur aliquis . . . . ut saluemini.

[CLXXV.] (*a*) In agenda mortuorum. (2 Mach. xii. 42–6.)
  Uir fortissimus Iuda . . . .
      . . . . a peccato soluerentur.

 (*b*) [Item.] (1 Thess. iv. 13–18.)
  Nolumus autem uos ignorare . . . .
      . . . . in uerbis istis.

CHAPTER I
The Sources

§ 1. IN approaching the Epistle-lists[a] it is natural to look first for one which can serve as a standard of comparison for all the rest. Happily, here, also, as in the case of the Gospel-lists, such a document is available, for it is found serving as the basis of a Corbie MS. now at Leningrad, which has been fully described by Staerk,[b] and is here called Corbie. From this MS. we can easily recover the 'Standard list', and use it as the norm with which all the other lists are compared. In this MS. the basic entries are consecutively numbered, and this numbering (in Roman figures) will serve us throughout. Only about half a dozen later additions have been made in this MS. to the basic S, namely, the 'Standard' list, and they are easily distinguished from it, as they bear no number. This state of things may be seen clearly in the print of the list which has been set at the head of this inquiry; see pp. 1–24.

Here, too, as in the case of the Gospels, the 'Standard' list is not the earliest one available. There is an 'Earlier' Epistle-list[c] existing which comes to us from the same Würzburg MS. which furnished the 'Earlier' Gospel-list. It is here called We. This MS. has been described already in connexion with its Gospel-capitulary (vol. II, p. 74): but it must also be noted here that the two lists which it contains are given separately, *i.e.* the Epistles and Gospels are not interwoven, as is done in the Comes MSS. (See below, Chap. V.)

There is also a third type of list available for consideration; it bears the name of Alcuin, and is therefore here called Alc. This is markedly different from either the 'Earlier' or the 'Standard' list. It has an enumeration of its own, which will be used, where necessary (in Arabic figures), to supplement the other (Roman) enumeration. These three representative lists must now be described.

The MS. which is taken as the source of the Standard Series of Epistles is Leningrad, Codex Q.v.1. No. 16, an Epistle-Lectionary of the 10th century,

---

[a] The word 'Epistle' must be taken to include all the lessons read at Mass other than those drawn from the Gospels.

[b] Dom A. Staerk, *Les MSS. Latins* &c., 2 vols. (Saint Peterbourg 1910.)

[c] Available only in this MS. It has been printed with valuable notes by Dom Morin in *R.B.* (1910), xxvii, pp. 41–74, reprinted separately, and also reproduced in *D.A.C.L.* viii. 2285 and ff.

Here the enumeration of this list is given as We with an Arabic figure in italic type.

formerly at Corbie perhaps, and later at S. Germain-des-Prés by Paris.[a] ff. 168. 201 × 135.

It has at the opening 'Sancti Hieronymi liber Comitis'; but this is probably a later addition.

At f. 1ᵛ is a short series of additional lessons: (*a*) for St. Agnes, *Qui gloriatur*, to which a reference is made in the main lectionary at No. XVIII; (*b*) for St. Cecilia, *De uirginibus autem* (1 Cor. vii. 25–34); (*c*) Nl. S. Benedict. *Qui custodierint justitiam* (selections from Sap. vi. 11–21); (*d*) Purification, *Ecce ego mittam* (Mal. iii. 1–4); (*e*) Cathedra Petri, *Petrus apostolus* (1 Pet. i. 1 with parts of iv and v); (*f*) *Dominus mihi astitit*, called 'Lectio Epistole b. Pauli ad Timotheum'. (2 Tim. iv. 17, 18.)

At f. 4ᵛ the pseudo-Hieronymian prologue is given, which will be discussed at a later stage. *Incipit prologus libri comitis S. Hieronimi Presbiteri missus ad Constantium.* Quamquam licenter . . . . &c.

At f. 6 is the List of liturgical days, which corresponds almost entirely with the headings of the main lectionary itself. It begins thus: 'INCIPIUNT CAPITULA LIBRI COMITIS I. In uigl. ntl. d. Ad nonam. Statio ad S. Mariam': and goes down to No. CLXXV, 'In agenda mortuorum.' Expliciunt capitula.

The blank pages ff. 10–11ᵛ are occupied by later additions, a Deprecation with short prayers, 'In spiritu humilitatis et in animo contrito' . . . . ending with (f. 11) a form of anathema and cursing. Then, overleaf, without heading, the lectionary itself begins, which is summarized above, pp. 1–24.

At the end of the Lectionary proper, further additions have been made. They are supplementary to the Standard series, and fall into two groups, neither of which has been found in other MSS. The first group runs on continuously with the Standard series thus:

In inuentione S. Crucis (Gal. vi. 8–14) Que enim seminauerit . . . . et ego mundo . . . .

In nat. S. Petri de Cathedra Deponentes igitur omnem malitiam. *Require eam Ebd. Pasche Feria vii ad Lateranis.* (LXXIV.)

In uigiliis omnium Apostolorum (Acts iv. 24–33) Leuauerunt vocem . . . . erat in omnibus illis.

In uigilia. In Adsumptione S. Mariae (Ecclus. xxiv. 20–8) Ego quasi myrra . . . . generatione seculorum.

In die passionis S. Johannis Baptiste (Is. xliii. 1–7) Hec dicit d. creans te . . . . et feci eum . . . .

Item in nat. S. Marie (Ezech. xliv. 1–4) Conuerti me ad uiam . . . . egredietur.

In nat. S. Maur[i]cii (Apoc. vi. 9–11) Vidi sub altare . . . . sicut et illi.

VIII KAL. AUG. Nat. S. Jacobi Apostoli (Eph. i. 3–7) = VI *a*.

The second group follows then after a space and in a later hand.

DOM. ANTE LXX SI NECESSE EST. (1 Tim. i. 15–17.) Fidelis sermo . . . . Christus uenit . . . . honor et gloria in s. s. Amen.

---

[a] See Staerk, vol. i, pp. 135–51, and facs. xxi; vol. ii, facs. lx.

The Sources

SANCTE CRUCIS. (Gal. vi. 11–14.) Videte qualibus litteris . . . . ego mundo.
Alia (Apoc. vii. 2–12). Et ecce ego Iohannes uidi alterum . . . . fortitudo
   D. n. in saecula saeculorum.
(1 Cor. xv. 51–7). Ecce mysterium uobis dico . . . . uictoriam
   per d. n. J. C.
(Apoc. xiv. 13, 14). Audiui uocem de celo . . . . Amodo . . . .
   opera enim illorum secuuntur illos.
(1 Cor. xv. 51–7). Ecce misterium . . . . *again.*
(1 Thess. iv. 13–18). Nolumus uos ignorare = CLXXV *b*.
This last entry repeats No. CLXXV *b*, the last item of the Standard set.

§ 2. The Earlier Series is available only in the Würzburg MS. (We) (University Library MS. Mp. th. fol. 62). ff. 16 (292 × 225), written in an 'insular' hand of the 8th century.

   f. 1ᵛ. A List of liturgical days; this corresponds very closely with the Epistle-list (i–ccxiii) following: it notes the Stations.
   f. 2ᵛ. The Epistle-list.
   f. 10ᵛ. The Gospel-list follows (see vol. II, p. 74, &c.).

See the full account of this document given with a valuable commentary by Morin in *R.B.*, *u.s.* It has an enumeration of its own which, of course, differs from the Standard list, and is here only utilized exceptionally. (We with roman figure in italic.)

There is no list known, other than this, which is anterior to the Stational Masses of the Thursdays in Lent. It seems to be subsequent to the Dedication of the Pantheon to St. Mary and the Martyrs, and thus it would represent the century between 608 and 731. But it should be noticed that the evidence derived from a reference to the Dedication of the Pantheon by Boniface IV (608–15) is to be found here, not in the direct form of an insertion of the festival itself of the Dedication at May 13 (Dedic. S. Marie ad martyres), but only in the indirect form of a note that the Station is held in that church on Friday in Easter week. ('Feria vi. ad S. Maria Martyra.') There is no similar note inserted at January 1, which is the one other occasion in the year on which the Station was usually held at the Pantheon, for there is no entry at all for that day. Further, it may be significant that, though the word 'martyra' is in the body of the epistle-lectionary, it is not in the corresponding place in the List of liturgical days which precedes the two lists. Possibly, therefore, it is here only as a scribal addition, and the Station intended on that day may have been originally held at S. Mary major, as on the Sunday previous. In that case the evidence for 608 as the *terminus a quo* for dating the MS. would disappear.

§ 3. The other Epistle-list available (Alc), which is so independent both of We and of S that it must be taken as representing a fresh type, is the well-known lectionary printed in outline by Tommasi[a] under the title 'Comes ab Albino ex Caroli Imperatoris praecepto emendatus'. Attention must be called to the actual details of the original MS.[b]

This high-sounding title is not in the MS.[c] Its contents are mainly two lists of Epistles, with a list of the liturgical days prefixed to each list.

f. 2. 'Incipiunt tituli lectionum sequentis libri.' (242 titles.)
f. 5^v. 'Incipiunt tituli aliarum lectionum &c.' (The 65 further titles.)
f. 6 is blank.
f. 6^v is the title-page of the book in gold capitals, followed by the main lectionary (ff. 6^v–125 = Tommasi, pp. 298–313) —the 242 Epistles.
f. 125^v is blank.
f. 126. 'Incipit praefatio.' 'Hunc codicem &c.' = p. 314.
f. 127. The Supplementary lectionary (ff. 127–59^v = pp. 314–18)—the 65 Epistles; followed by 'Explicit'.
f. 160 has the additional entry for St. Luke (p. 318).
f. 160^v has the later addition for the B. V. Mary.
The Epistle to Constantius—'Quanquam licenter &c.' (p. 319), is not included in the MS.

The enumeration in this MS. is unlike either of the two enumerations above-mentioned. It is utilized in this Study, to identify entries in the Main Lectionary or its Appendix, which are not in the two previous types, in the form A or AA, with an Arabic numeral.

This document when once printed by Tommasi acquired a great fame, which contrasts with the small influence that (so far as present evidence goes) it seems to have had in its own time, or on the development subsequently. The discussion of it in detail is deferred until the significance of the other two types has been described.

[a] *Opera*, v. 297–318, cp. *D.A.C.L.* v. 300–11.
[b] Paris, Bibl. Ntle. MS. Fonds Latin 9452. ff. 160. 270×215.
[c] It represents a deduction from the statement made in the preface to the Appendix at f. 127.

CHAPTER II

A Comparison of the Earlier Series with the Standard Series

§ 1. AFTER the heading (in We only) 'Incipiunt capitula lectionum de circulo anni' the openings vary slightly. The Earlier Series (We) differs from S, the Standard, (*a*) in having I *a*, assigned to the Christmas vigil, placed at the end, and not at the beginning, of the list. (*b*) In putting its four Christmas epistles together before the three Old Test. lessons, so that I–IV are followed by II *a*, III *a*, IV *a*.

§ 2. There is soon noticeable in We the tendency to group several entries for a class of Saint round some conspicuous festival, which is found also in the *Leonianum* Sacramentary. Thus, at VI two further lessons are added in We, one O.T. and one N.T. Later on they figure in the Commune of S as CLI *a* and CXLVIII *a*. Similarly, at December 31, St. Silvester's day, CL *b* and *c* are inserted followed by CXLVII *b*. The way is being prepared for the emergence of a Commune Sanctorum.

§ 3. We has no Oct Nativ, VIII, as such, nor Vig Theoph, X: for Theoph itself III is given as well as XI. Then follow four entries 'post Theophania' which are in S the Sundays XII, XIV, XV, XVI.

§ 4. Next, St. Sebastian (*We 24*) has two lessons, CLIII *c* as well as XXIV.

§ 5. Then come, belated, four entries 'Post nat. domini' $^{1-4}$: they are VIII and IX of S with *Fidelis sermo*, Alc 16, and *Considerate apostolum*, Alc 17.

§ 6. A group of four lessons for Virgins follows with the heading 'In nat. SS. Agnae et Agathae', XVIII, with CXVIII, CLIV *a* and *b* as well (*We 30–3*). Thus, in the early part of the year the provision for Sundays is doubly peculiar. S adopted those for the four Sundays after Epiphany, and kept two of the four provided after Christmas for Oct Nativ, and Nativ¹, while Alc took the two others for Theoph².³.

§ 7. From Septuagesima to Low Sunday We and S are alike except that:

(*a*) besides the Lenten Thursdays,[a] L v, L vii, and XL⁵vii are absent from We.

(*b*) On the Ember Saturday We provides an additional epistle called 50 'Item alia unde supra' Rogamus et obsecramus: it subsequently is utilized for the 'Vacat' Sunday following: see

[a] At XLIII of We read feria IV for feria V.

xxxiii. Similar procedure is also evident at other 'Vacat' Sundays: see § 10.

(c) at XL⁴ We has the heading 'Dominica ante XXma. ad Hierusalem': while at XL⁴vii S adds 'in aurium apertione', which is not in We. At XL⁵ 'in mediana', probably by mistake, takes the place of 'in XVma'.

(d) at XL⁵vi the Station is correctly given as 'Ad S. Stephanum': at Maundy Thursday We adds 'Ad Lateranis'.

(e) The rubric following LXI a is not in We, nor yet the list of vigil-lessons for Easter Even—numbered for our purposes LXVI* because it is unnumbered in S.

§ 8. (a) At Eastertide (*We 58*) to LXXV We adds the Station 'Ad Lateranis' but omits the title.

(b) At LXXVIII We does not provide for SS. Philip and James day at its chronological place: it has been attracted away and grouped round SS. Peter and Paul, with *Unicuique nostrum* CXLVIII b prefixed to LXXVIII *Stabunt iusti*. At LXXX We lacks the Invention of the Cross.

(c) In We nine Sundays (*We 94–102*) are set down in order for 'post Oct. Paschae'. Five of these remain on in S while Oct Pasch⁶⁻⁸ of We appear in S as Pent²⁻⁴: and the last of the nine becomes Pent⁶ in S. See further at § 18. It is noticeable that here, also, the provision of Sundays at first was peculiar and excessive.

(d) Litania maior in both types is placed at the Gallican, not the Roman date: but We has no Vigil Asc.

§ 9. At the Vigil on Whitsun-eve as at Easter Even, the vigil-lessons are wanting in We.

After Whit Sunday and its week comes a Sunday called 'Dom. in nat. sanctorum', with two lessons (*We 114, 115*) from the Apocalypse:

(a) Vidi ostium apertum, which begins like XCIV (Rev. iv. 1) but ends with Rev. vii. 9–12. This use of XCIV here explains the appearance of XCIV subsequently in S as Pent¹.

(b) Item unde supra. Respondit unus de senioribus (Rev. vii. 13–17) .... ab oculis eorum. Thus (b) fits on to (a) and there is no XCIV a.

These entries recall the Eastern custom of celebrating an All-Saints festival on this day.ᵃ They imply also that there was at this point no 'Vacat' Sunday after an ordination.

ᵃ See Morin's note in *R.B.*, *u.s.* Note also that in Agimund's Homiliary of the 8th century, hailing from the Church of the Twelve Apostles in Rome, the second volume ends after the Com. of St. Paul with two homilies 'de nat. Apostolorum'. See *Römische Quartalschrift*, 1929, i–ii.

A Comparison of Earlier Series with Standard Series

§ 10. Naturally, therefore, Ember week does not coincide with Whit-week. In We it immediately follows the All-Saints Sunday at Oct Pent, while S has it after Pent³: but as We gives no set of Sundays for the summer, this difference may be more apparent than real. The only other such Sundays included here in We are those following the Ember days.

(a) At Sabb. Mens. quarti the additional epistle provided in We is *124* 'Ubi supra' Existimo quia (Rom. viii. 8–13).

The rubric again is very vague, as in § 7(b): but this *Existimo* epistle must equally have been passed on to the 'Vacat' Sunday. This is clear from Alc where it has the same place 136, but a more definite rubric— 'Dominica ut supra'. It is followed by Pent³, thus showing that the 'Vacat' Sunday which took over this epistle was Pent².

In S, however, the *Existimo* epistle does not appear till Pent⁵, though the Ember Week is placed after Pent³. This late position of that epistle was probably the result of the intercalation of fresh Sundays between Pentecost and the feast of SS. Peter and Paul. (See p. 35.)

(b) In September We has Michaelmas inserted before the additional epistle *153* (*Gratias ego*): but the old vague rubric 'Cuius supra' is left unaltered in We. In Alc it runs 'Dominica ut supra mensis Septimi' showing that there (as also in S cxxix Pent¹⁹) it has gone to fill the 'Vacat' Sunday.

(c) In December We puts four of its five Advent Sundays between the Saturday and the Epistle *174 Gaudete in domino* which must once have been the alternative Epistle of Saturday but has now gone definitely to be the Epistle of the 'Vacat' Sunday with the rubric 'De adventu domini'.

§ 11. The plan of the Ember days themselves shows some differences. We has no lesson from Daniel. It adds two lessons, however, for the September Saturday, inserting (*146*) between (a) and (b) of cxxviii the lesson Conteram iugum ... (Jer. xxviii. 4 and xxx. 8–11) ... ut saluem te: and after (d) the lesson (*150*) Orauit moyses ... (Exod. xxxii. 11–14) ... aduersus populum suum.

Again, in Advent, between (c) and (d) of cxlv We inserts (*167*) Ecce seruus m. (Is xlii. 1–9) ... ego annuntio. ...

§ 12. Note the grouping together in We at SS. John and Paul of cxlvii*a*, cxlviii, and cix, and after St. Paul of cxlviii*b* and lxxviii. We has no Felicitas, cxiv, but gives two lessons cli*e* and cli*a* to Sixtus.

32 A Comparison of Earlier Series with Standard Series

Four lessons are collected at St. Lawrence, that is, CXLIX and CLI*d* as well as the usual CXVI, CXVII, and they are differently assigned. Thereafter we miss in We CXVIII and CXX, and have no Saints-day till Michaelmas. We is generous to St. Andrew giving VI*a* and CXLVII*b* for the vigil as well as the normal two for the Day.

Finally, it is to be noted that none of the extra feasts,[a] which have been added in the Corbie MS. to the Standard, was derived from We apart from S.

§ 13. A noteworthy feature of the Early Series is the placing of the Dedication Festival immediately before the Vigil of St. Andrew and not in the Votive section, thus *(154–6)*: In Dedicatione ecclesiae', Nos. CLIX*b* and CLIX*a*, followed by 'In Dedicatione oratorii', with No. CLX. This may have some connexion with the fact that Nov. 16 was the 'Dedicatio basilicarum Apostolorum Petri et Pauli' according to the Kalendar of the Vatican Servicebooks.[b] There is, however, another entry, 'In dedicatione aecclesiae' added in We (as *213*) at the end of the Votive section with Conuertit rex Salomon (3 Reg. viii. 14–34) . . . patribus eorum d. D. noster.

§ 14. The section in We containing Advent is, as already noted, preceded by the Advent Ember days. Then provision is made for five Sundays in Advent (CXL, CXXXIX, CXLI, CXLII, and CXLVI). This is followed by 'In vigilias domini' which is No. 1 in the Standard series. Thus, the absence from We of the series of Sundays after Pentecost (Pent^1–Pent^{25}) is among its most marked differences from the Standard series.

§ 15. We has no formal Commune sanctorum to correspond with the section in S containing CXLVII–CLIV. Votives follow at once after Advent, as described above; the Ordination Services *(176)*, CLV–CLVII*a* and *b*; and for the 'Natale Papae' *(180–)*, no less than seven entries. First comes Jeiunauit Esdras (2 Esd. i. 4–11 adapted) . . . populo tuo for the Vigil: and for the Day itself CLVIII*c* with CL*a* and CLVIII*a* and *b*. Then there follow two more: first another Pronuntiabunt leuitae . . . . suscitauit te . . . . manuum tuarum,[c] which is a compound lesson from Deuteronomy (xxvii. 14 and xxviii. 9–12), though called Leviticus; and finally *(186)* Ego tuli te (= No. CLXI 'In adventu episcopi'). Then comes 'Ad sponsas uelandas' with CLXII, and also Volo uos sine sollicitudine esse (1 Cor. vii. 32–5) . . . . obsecrandi.

[a] See pp. 15–18.
[b] See Tommasi, *Opera*, vol. iv. 15, the Antiphonal of the Vatican.
[c] Cp. CLVIII*b*.

A Comparison of Earlier Series with Standard Series

§ 16. The next five entries form a sort of rudimentary Commune sanctorum (*189–93*) under the heading 'In nat. Sanctorum'. They are in more or less degree identified with Nos. CLI*b*, CLIII*a*, CLII*b*, CLIII*b*, and CLII*a* of the Standard series.

There follows In nat. S. Sabinae *Mulierem fortem* (= CXIV for St. Felicitas).

§ 17. In the Votive section, which begins at *We 195*, six entries are found for 'In laetania tempore belli' Nos. CLXIV *a* and *b*. *Egrotauit Ezechias* = No. XXIII, for L v; *Factum est uerbum* = No. XLIV, for XL³v; then CLXIV*c*, and finally Unusquisque se a proximo (Jer. ix. 4–9) . . . . ulciscitur anima mea. 'In sterelitate pluuiae' has CLXVII, with the addition of Factum est uerbum (Jer. ii. 1–7; xlii. 12) . . . . Surge et descende . . . . miserebor uestri . . . . and CLXVI.

'In die belli' has Facite iudicium (Jer. xxii. 3, 4): (Alc 221) . . . . populus eorum: with CLXV*a* and *b*. Then—to judge from the numbering—three entries (*207–9*) are missing.[a] There follows 'Item ut supra' Principes et satrapae (Dan. vi. 16–23) . . . . magnus es d. D. Danielis. We now reach the 'In agendis' which has only CLXXV*a* with *Facta est super me* = LXVI* *h*. Then the series of appropriated lessons ends with the addition for the Dedication Festival already mentioned in § 13 as *213*.

§ 18. There follows one of the most interesting and unusual features of We. It gives from *214* to *255* a set of forty-two lessons, drawn from the Pauline epistles, unappropriated to any special occasions, and representing a plan of more or less continuous reading: six from Romans, three from 1 Corinthians,[b] four from 2 Corinthians, and so on. Alc has similarly a short list (Alc 234–42) headed 'Incipiunt lectiones quotidianis diebus'. When these are entered in tabular form[c] with references to their subsequent appropriation, it becomes clear that the first section of the We list has mainly provided the set of Epistles which later was assigned to the Sundays from Pent[5] to Pent[25] in S; or from Apost[1] to Ang[6] in Alc. There are certain exceptions, but they can be explained.

First it is necessary to recall that the Epistles which were allotted to the 'Vacat' Sundays after Embertides, when they became liturgical days, were settled before any lessons were

[a] Morin notes that they figure in the List of Liturgical Days with heading 'Item ut supra'.

[b] One is wrongly entered as from the Epistle to the Romans.

[c] Both these sets are placed in the table (p. 34): and so are the relevant items in the Alcuinian Appendix (marked AA).

TABLE OF WE'S UNAPPROPRIATED EPISTLES

Earlier Series, We		Standard		Alcuin
[123]	Rom. v. 1–5	xcviii*	Pent³vii =	135
214	6–11			234 Quotid
215	18–21			148 Apost¹
216	vi. 3–11	cviii	Pent⁷	149 Apost²
217	19–23	cx	Pent⁸	150 Apost³
218	viii. 1–6			151 Apost⁴
219	12–17	cxi	Pent⁹	152 Apost⁵
[124]	18–23	c	Pent⁵ =	136 Pent⁵
220	1 Cor. x. 6–13	cxii	Pent¹⁰	AA 22
221	xii. 2–11	cxiii	Pent¹¹	126 Oct Pent
		cxv	ªPent¹²	
222	xv. 39–46			162 Lawr¹
223	2 Cor. iii. 4–7	cxix	Pent¹³	235 Quotid
224	iv. 5–10			AA 24
225	v. 1–11			163 Lawr²
226	vi. 14–vii. 1			164 Lawr³
227	Gal. iii. 16–22	cxxi	Pent¹⁴	165 Lawr⁴
228	v. 16–24	cxxii	Pent¹⁵	166 Lawr⁵
229	v. 25–vi. 10	cxxiii	Pent¹⁶	236 Quotid
230	Eph. iii. 13–21	cxxiv	Pent¹⁷	AA 26
231	iv. 1–6	cxxv	Pent¹⁸	167
[153]		cxxix	Pent¹⁹	[177]
232	23–8	cxxxi	Pent²⁰	183 Ang¹ = 237 Quotid
233	v. 15–21	cxxxii	Pent²¹	184 Ang²
234	vi. 10–17	cxxxiii	Pent²²	185 Ang³
235	Phil. i. 6–11	cxxxiv	Pent²³	186 Ang⁴ = 238 Quotid
236	iii. 17–21	cxxxv	Pent²⁴	187 Ang⁵ (to iv. 3)
237	Col. i. 9–14	cxxxvi	Pent²⁵ (to 11)	188 Ang⁶ (to ver. 14)
238	12–18			AA. 25. Ang⁶ in Aud.
239	ii. 8–13			239 Quotid. Theoph⁵ in Aud.
240	iii. 5–11			AA 17. Ang⁷ in Aud. Val.
241	12–17			Ang⁸ in Val.
[174]	iv. 4–7	cxlvi	Nativ¹	[208]
242	1 Thess. ii. 9–13			Ang⁸ in Aud.
243	2 Thess. ii. 15–iii. 5			240 Quotid
244	iii. 6–13			AA 27
245	1 Tim. i. 3–14			
246	ii. 1–7	clxix	In adv. jud.	225 & 113 Lit maior (b).
247	vi. 7–14			
248	2 Tim. i. 8–13			20
249	ii. 22–iii. 15			
250	Hebr. i. 13–ii. 3			
251	x. 32–8	cliii	d	
252	iv. 11–16			cp. AA 32
253	xii. 3–9			
254	12–23			
255	xiii. 17–21			AA 9 for Oct Pasch iv

ª Note that S for Pent¹² has taken verses 1–10 of 1 Cor. xv instead of verses 39–46.

A Comparison of Earlier Series with Standard Series

assigned to the other Sundays of the summer. These, therefore, do not appear in We's list of Unappropriated lessons. They are here in the Table, but enclosed in brackets. When the full set for Sundays was made out, they retained their places. The former fell into line at Pent[5] in S(or at Pent[2] in Alc, owing to the differing dating of the Embertide there. The latter came into line at Pent[19] in S(or at the Sunday before Ang[1] in Alc). When this fact is taken into account, it is clear that both in S and Alc the vacant places in the latter part of the summer were filled up by a process of selection from some list of Unappropriated passages which was very similar to that preserved in We.

The selection was differently made in S and in Alc, but in neither of these cases did the selector go farther down the list than the entry Col. i. 9–11; and in regard to the last six passages chosen, both the selectors agreed. There are signs in other MSS. that other selectors, following the same or a similar list, went a little farther down it;[a] but, even so, most of the second half of the list was apparently unutilized for this purpose.

Further, it is noticeable that the list itself ignored all the Catholic Epistles—no doubt, because they had been largely, though not systematically, used in Eastertide.

This explanation does not account for the Epistles of the earlier Sundays after Pentecost. Now the early Gospel-lists have shown[b] that originally there were only two reckoned after Pentecost, and that three or four were subsequently added in June,[c] *i.e.* previous to Apost[1]. The same thing seems to have happened with the Epistles, though the proof in this case is inferential, not documentary.

When subsequently it was desired to provide for further Sundays early after Pent, recourse for the epistles was had, not to We's list, but to those passages of the Catholic Epistles which, in practice, were by then unused because the Sundays to which they had been originally allotted were superfluous Sundays— Pasch[6–9]. (See § 8 *c.*) Both S and Alc took this line, but carried it out differently. The two following tables show the disposition.

Apart from the 'Vacat' Sunday (as described above), the Standard added four—two from 1 John, and two from 1 Peter. Alc added only two before having recourse again to the Unappropriated series, for the Epistle of Apost[1]. The Standard does not

---

[a] See the italicized entries in the Table taken from MSS. Aud and Val.
[b] Vol. II, p. 69.
[c] Vol. II, p. 113.

36 *A Comparison of Earlier Series with Standard Series*

have recourse thither till the next Sunday, Pent⁷ = Apost² as the previous table (p. 34) shows. So the two types reunite.

THE ADDED SUNDAYS AFTER PENTECOST

Earlier Series, We	Standard	Alcuin
Dom. in Natl. ss.*114* Apoc. iv and vii	Oct Pent (xciv) Apoc. iv. 1–9	Oct Pent (126) 1 Cor. xii. 2–11 = cxiii
	Pent² (xcv) 1 Jo. iv. 16–21 (A 138)	'Dom. ut S' (136) = c
	Pent³ (xcvi) 1 Jo. iii. 13–18	Pent³ (137) 1 Pet. iv. 7–11 = lxxxv AA 18
	Pent⁴ (xcix) 1 Pet. v. 6–11	Pent⁴ (138) 1 Jo. iv. 16–21 = xcv
'Ubi supra' (*124*) =	Pent⁵ (c) Rom. viii. 18–23	Apost¹ (148) Rom. v. 18–21
	Pent⁶ (ciii) 1 Pet. iii. 8–15	
	Pent⁷ (cviii) Rom. vi. 3–11 =	Apost² = cviii

It will further illustrate the methods employed to give a table of the use which had already previously been made of the Catholic Epistles, arranged in biblical order.

TABLE OF CATHOLIC EPISTLES

	Earlier Series, We			Standard	Alcuin
92	1 Pet. ii	1–10	Pasch vii	= lxxiv	= 99
95		11–20	Oct Pasch²	= lxxvi	= 103
		21–5	Oct Pasch¹	= lxvi	= 102
102	iii	8–15	Oct Pasch⁹	ciii Pent⁶	AA 21
91		18–22	Pasch vi	= lxxiii	= 98
98	iv	7–11	Oct Pasch⁵	= lxxxv	
101	v	6–11	Oct Pasch⁸	xcix Pent⁴	
96	James i	17–21	Oct Pasch³	= lxxix	= 104
97		22–7	Oct Pasch⁴	= lxxxi	= 111
103	v	16–20	Litania m.	= lxxxii	= 112
100	1 Jo. iii	13–18	Oct Pasch⁷	xcvi Pent³	AA 18
99	iv	16–21	Oct Pasch⁶	xcv Pent²	138 Pent⁴
93	v	4–10	Oct Pasch	= lxxv	= 100

This suggests that Pent²⁻⁴ were taken over direct by S from We when they were no longer required for Oct Pasch⁶⁻⁸, and after the 'Vacat' Sunday had been settled into the series as Pent⁵.

§ 19. This detailed comparison of We with the Standard series of Epistles has brought out a number of features which justify the title 'Earlier Series' given to We. The principal ones are the following:

(*a*) The Sundays. We exhibits a disorderly stage in which spare Sundays are grouped after Christmas (4) and Easter (9), and perhaps after Epiphany (4): but this grouping is crude; and there is none after Pentecost.

(*b*) The Common of Saints. This, also, is in an inchoate stage in We, while in the Standard it is regularly organized.

(*c*) The Saints-days, entered individually in We, include four which are not in the Standard. This, however, is probably due, not to having a fuller Kalendar, but to the lack of an adequate Commune.

(*d*) The absence of provision in We for the Thursdays in Lent and other days of later origin is perhaps the clearest of the distinctive features.

(*e*) The supplemental list of Unappropriated Epistles harks back to a stage which more or less immediately precedes the allocation of any particular passages to the Sundays between Pentecost and Advent. Up till then special or fixed provision had not been made.

There is a notable gap in We's list between Rom. viii and 1 Cor. x. It is explained by the use of Rom. xii–xv for Theoph [1-4] and Adv [1, 2].

§ 20. An interesting comparison may now be drawn between the method of the Earlier Epistle-list as represented so far, in its general outline, and the method of the Earlier Gospel-list as shown in vol. II, chapters II and III.

The two lists are far from being harmonious. They seem to have grown up independently of one another, and to develop without much reference one to another. Each led its own life apart, until the emergence, first of the 'Comes', and later of the 'Missale plenum', made them bedfellows in the same volume, and compelled them to some concordance. Throughout their existence the Epistle-lists remained in some respects less developed than the Gospel-lists, both in their contents and in their method, though in other respects—*e.g.* the Commune Sanctorum—they seem ahead.

(*a*) There is no stage in the Gospel-lists so disorderly as that which We exhibits in regard to Sundays: but in the Gospel usage, too, there were, at first, such anomalies as the provision of too many Sundays (10) after Epiphany, and too few (20) after Pentecost. (See vol. I, chapter iii, and the parallel case of the Epistles argued at p. 35.)

(*b*) The rise of the Commune, which the We shows in an inchoate stage comparable to the Leonine Sacramentary, seems to come in and mature at an earlier stage in the Epistle-book than in the Gospel-book.

(c) Perhaps in consequence of this, the number of Saints-days entered individually in the Epistle-book remains continuously far less than in the Gospel-book.

(d) Lent preserves an old terminology in the Epistle-list, which is common to We and the Standard series, but is not customary in Gospel-books. The first Sunday is, quite properly, 'Quadragesima', the third is 'Tricesima', the fourth is '(Ante) Vicesima', while the ensuing week is 'In mediana'. The fifth Sunday is 'in XVma' (or 'in Mediana', We). Palm Sunday is 'Dominica Indulgentia'.

(e) Litania maior is only very rarely found at the Roman position in April: normally it is inserted just before Ascension—as it should be according to the Sequence of Epistles.[a]

(f) In Epistle-lists it is usual to find five Sundays reckoned as in Advent.

(g) Perhaps the most remarkable contrast between the Epistle-series and the Gospel-series is the absence from the Standard of any Epistles for week-days. Some such provision was only slowly and subsequently added as time went on, and it never became as full or as uniform a provision as that of the Gospel-books, as will appear hereafter.

(h) This difference largely accounts for the difference in size of the two sets. There are 272 Gospels provided for the yearly course as against the 146 sections provided in the Epistle-list. Some of these latter sections, it is true, contain two or more single entries, as follows:

    (i) At Christmas-time there is an Old Testament lesson as well as Epistle. (See Nos. I–IV, VI.)

    (ii) At each Ember season there are two O.T. lessons provided for the Wednesday, and for the Saturday five O.T. lessons besides the Epistle.

    (iii) At Mid-Lent XL^{4}iv has one lesson from O.T. and another from N.T.; and XL^{4}vii has two O.T. lessons.

    (iv) In Holy Week each week-day has two O.T. lessons, except Maundy Thursday and Easter Even.

    (v) Then the Vigil has its full set of twelve O.T. lessons, with the four associated canticles, besides the Epistle for Mass.

    (vi) The Vigil of Pentecost is similar, but the number of lessons is reduced to six, with three canticles.

[a] See Table above, p. 36, but the choice of this passage may be merely topical, in reference to harvest. Alc has also 113 = CLXIX, which has a more general reference to prayer.

A Comparison of Earlier Series with Standard Series

(vii) After Pentecost two O.T. lessons are provided for the Wednesday and for the Octave.

But even when allowance is made for these extras, the difference in size between the two lists remains considerable.

(*j*) The rest of the difference of size in the two lists is explained by noting the set of Saints-days included in them. The Standard Epistle-list has only 22 such entries as against 97 in the Standard Gospel-list. The two lists, however, in practice could be made to correspond, for the most part, by using the Commune, containing 30 entries, which the Epistle-list contains, but the Gospel-list does not. This would provide for most of the days lacking. But there was nothing suitable for the Purification, Annunciation, or the Nativity of the B.V.M. (unless by adopting the lesson for the Assumption No. cxviii);[a] nor for the Exaltation of Holy Cross, except by referring to the Invention, which is in the Standard Epistle-list as No. lxxx, though not in the Standard Gospel-list; nor for St. Peter's Chains, except by reference to SS. Peter and Paul or else to the Octave; nor for the Pascha Annotina.

In this way, however, the provision for Saints through the Commune was in reality more ample in the Epistle-list than it was subsequently in the Gospel-list; for there, when the Gospels suitable for general use came to be gathered together from the series of individual entries of Saints-days to form a Commune, it started with no more than 12 items, and did not ever much exceed 20. (See vol. II, pp. 107, 109.)

(*k*) Other points of interest also emerge from a comparison of the two lists of saints:

(1) As to the feasts of the blessed Virgin[b] We has none, the Standard has only the Assumption: the Nativity is among the additions made in the Corbie MS. of the Standard series; the Purification and Annunciation come in first with the 'Alcuinian' revision.

(2) As to the feasts of Holy Cross, the Standard list has only the Invention May 3 (it is not in We), but not the Exaltation, which appears first among the additions to the Corbie MS.

(3) The plan of joining SS. Agnes and Agatha is common to We and the Standard, but contrary to the use of the Gospel-books.

(4) The observance of a separate Vigil of St. Paul (in We only) has a Gelasian flavour.

[a] This is directed in the Corbie MS. called S at the addition for the Nativity.
[b] See vol. I, pp. 68–70.

(5) St. Felicitas at August 1 recalls the Machabees and her connexion with them; and again we taste a Gelasian flavour.

The conclusion of the matter is that the difference between Epistle-list and Gospel-list is not so great in substance and in working as it seems to be at first sight. If the Epistle-list was supplemented by a full Kalendar of the Saints-days to be observed, with references as to the use of the Commune, the two could be brought into harmony, provided that the Epistle of the Sunday was taken to serve for all the vacant days of the week following.

CHAPTER III
Alcuin's Lectionary

§ 1. THE third type of lectionary (Alc) already noted at p. 25, must now be more fully described. The Main Lectionary, to which the Appendix has been added, is not simply an enlarged form of the Standard series, for it exhibits some radical differences, as well as some minor variants, and much enlargement.

(*a*) The opening entries give several examples of minor variation:[a] I*a* of the Standard is lacking here, because it is given in Alc as No. 211, at the end of the year. 'In vigilia domini, ad nonam' III is set for Vig Theoph; III*a* and IV*a* are only to be found in the Appendix of Alc as AA 2 and AA 1: while VI*a* is set in Alc as A 195 in place of CXXXVII for the Vigil of St. Andrew.

(*b*) More serious variation is observed in the arrangement of Sundays. The Standard provides one Sunday after Christmas and four after Epiphany. Alc has

  9 Nativ¹ with XIV.
12 Nativ² with IX.
15 Theoph¹ with XII.
16 Theoph². Fidelis sermo et (1 Tim. i. 15–17) .... in saec. s. a.
17 Theoph³. Considerate apostolum (Heb. iii. 1–6) .... retineamus.
18 Theoph⁴ = XV.
19 Theoph⁵ = XVI.
20 Item alia Noli erubescere (2 Tim. i. 8–13) .... et dilectione in C. J. d. n.

(*c*) As to Saints-days Silvester follows Nativ¹ with 10, 11 =

---

[a] The Roman numerals refer to the Standard list; the Arabic to Alcuin's lectionary, and, when AA is prefixed, to its Appendix. Italics show a passage which has appeared already, but differently placed.

Alcuin's Lectionary

CL, CL*a*. After the above group of Sundays comes a group of 8 feasts thus:
    21 Felix CL*c*. 22 Marcellus CLI*a*. 23 Sebastian, as S.
    24 Agnes in place of Agnes and Agatha XVIII.
    25 'In die qua beata virgo offerebat Christum in templo' Ecce ego mittam (Mal. iii. 1–4) . . . . anni antiqui.
    26 Agatha CXVIII.   27 Valentine CXLVII*b*.
    28 In adnunciacione S. Mariae *Egredietur virgo* = CXLIV.

(*d*) In Lent the following points deserve notice in Alc. Septuagesima lacks its Station: so also XL² and the Thursdays. There is no L v, nor L vii.[a] The Thursdays differ from the Standard set thus:
    39 XL¹v. Orauit Esdras dicens, Quaeso (2 Esdr. i. 5–11) . . . . da misericordiam populo tuo, d. D. n.
    50 XL²v. *Misericordiae d.* = CLXV*b*.
    57 XL³v. Beatus vir qui confidit (Jer. xvii. 7–10) . . . . adinuentionum suarum.
    In the margin is added *Sta in porta*, i.e. XLIV.
    64 XL⁴v. Helisaeus aegrotabat (4 Reg. xiii. 14–21) . . . . pedes suos.
    73 XL⁵v. *Verbum quod factum* = XLIV.
    Note also 75 XL⁵vii has Exulta satis (Zach. ix. 9–16) . . . . saluabit eos.

(*e*) At Easter Even the rubric runs 'Expliciunt lectiones de quadragesima' 'Incipiunt lectiones de vig. Paschae'. The set of lessons is shorter here than in S; it is numbered separately 86–91, six entries only; = LXVI* *a, d, j*, with Canticle *Vinea*;[b] LXVI* *n, f*, with the 'Lectio' of Daniel *Angelus d. descendit* = XXXII *e*.
    Then 'Incipiunt lectiones de Pascha' with LXVII.
    Low Sunday is followed by 'De Pascha Annotina' with
    101 Non cesso gratias (Eph. i. 16–21) . . . . in futuro.
The saints of Eastertide follow on after 104 Oct Pasch³:
    105 SS. Philip and James Exurgens princeps (Acts v. 17–21) . . . . et docebant.
    106 St. Pancras CXLVII*a* followed by
    107–10 'In nat. Sanctorum', = CIX; CLII*a, b*; CLIII*a*.
After Oct Pasch⁴ comes 'Litania maior' with LXXXII, and also CLXIX as well.
    116 (Asc¹) has Deus qui diues (Eph. ii. 4–7) . . . . super nos in C. J.
    117 Vig Pent has only one entry,[c] the Epistle, LXXXVI *h*.

---

[a] Part of the Lesson XXIII is at Alc 219 'In die belli'.
[b] But *b, c* are in the Appendix as AA 5, 6.
[c] Two more, *viz.* LXVI**g, h*, are in the Appendix as AA 7, 8.

(*f*) After Pentecost the differences of Alc from S are more marked.

128–35, Ember days, are in the second week, preceded by 126 Oct Pent with CXIII instead of XCIV.

127 Marcellinus and Peter with Respondit unus de s. (Apoc. vii. 13–17) .... ex oculis eorum.

Then Sundays are resumed: 137 Pent³ LXXXV, and 138 Pent⁴ XCV.

Then a block of Saints-days:

139 Gervasius and Protasius XLVIII *c*.

140 John and Paul, Quis nos separabit (Rom. viii. 35–9) .... a caritate dei &c.

141–6 = CI, CII; CIV–CVII. (John B: Peter and Paul).

147 Oct Apostolorum, Deus personam (Gal. ii. 6–10) .... ipsum facere.

Then Sundays again: 148–52, five 'post nat. Apostolorum'. See the Table on p. 34.

148 Apost¹. Sicut per unius (Rom. v. 18–21) .... in vitam eternam ....

149 Apost² = CVIII.

150 Apost³ = CX.

151 Apost⁴. Nihil nunc damnationis (Rom. viii. 1–6) .... vita et pax ....

152 Apost⁵ = CXI.

Feasts again alternate in blocks with blocks of Sundays.

153 Sixtus CLI *e*.

154, 155 Lawrence CXVI, CXVII.

No Assumption, CXVIII, is included, but there follows a group of three unallotted passages for Saints:

156 'In nat. Sanctorum' Vidi ostium .... Ecce turba (Apoc. iv. 1; vii. 9–12) .... fortitudo deo n. in s. saec. with 157 = LXXVIII, and 158 CLIII *c*.

159 Cornelius and Cyprian CLIII *a*.

160 'In nat. Euangelistarum' with XCIV.

161 'In Decollatione S. Joh. B.' differs from S (CXX) in having: Sancti ludibria (Heb. xi. 36–9) .... probati inuenti sunt in ....

The next block of Sundays is reckoned from St. Lawrence, and differs from S, as has been shown above.

162 Lawr¹. Non omnis caro (1 Cor. xv. 39–46) .... quod spiritale.

163 Lawr². Scimus quoniam si terrestris (2 Cor. v. 1–11) .... nos esse per ....

164 Lawr³. Nolite iugum ducere (2 Cor. vi. 14–vii. 1) . . . . in timore dei.
165 Lawr⁴ = cxxi.   166 Lawr⁵ = cxxii.
167 'Hebdom. 1. mensis Sept.' = cxxv. Followed by the Ember days, 168–176, and
177 'Dom. ut supra mensis Sept.' = cxxix.

Three lessons 'in festivitate S. Mariae' follow next: 178 = cxiv;
179 Ego quasi vitis (Ecclus. xxiv. 23–31) . . . . vitam eternam habebunt;
180 = cliv d.

Then Michaelmas ('In Dedicatione basilicae S. Angeli') which has 181 = cxxx: and also
182 Et factum est praelium (Apoc. xii. 7–12) . . . . in eis.

It is followed by six Sundays (183–8), which correspond with cxxxi–cxxxvi: then another set of Saints:
189 Vigil of All Saints. Et ecce ego Johannes vidi in medio (Apoc. v. 6–12) . . . . et benedictionem in s. saec.
190 All Saints Day. Et ecce ego J. vidi alterum (Apoc. vii. 2–12) . . . . deo nostro in s. saec.
191 Vigil of St. Martin cli d: and 192 Feast cl a.
193 Cecilia, cliv b.   194 Clement, cli b.
195 Vigil of St. Andrew, not cxxxvii, but vi a: and
196 Feast cxxxviii.

Four Sundays are reckoned 'ante nat. domini': they are as usual 197–9 = cxl–cxlii, followed by 200–7 the normal Ember days and 208 the fourth Sunday cxlvi with two alternatives added, 'Item ut supra':
209 Nolite amittere (Heb. x. 35–9) . . . . in adquisitione animae.
210 which is cxxxix, usually the 5th Sunday before Christmas: and finally 'In vigiliis domini ad nonam' 211 = I a.

(g) The Votives which follow are these: clv, clvi, clvii b, clix a, clviii c and a, clxii. Thereafter comes divergence.
219 'In die belli' *Aegrotauit Ezechias* cp. xxiii.
220 'Item ut supra' = clxiv c.
221 'Item ut supra' Facite iudicium (Jer. xxii. 3, 4) . . . . populi eorum, ait . . . .
222 'In sterilitate pluuiae', clxvi.
223 'Pro aeris temperantia', Noli timere terra (Joel ii. 21–6) . . . . fecit nobiscum mirabilia.
224 'In tribulatione', Si iniquitates (Jer. xiv. 7–9) . . . . ne derelinquas nos, d. D. n.

225 'In aduentu iudicum' = CLXIX.

(*h*) There follows a rudimentary Commune:
>226 'In nat. Sacerdotum'. Scietis quia misi (Mal. ii. 4–7) .... exercituum est.
>227 'In nat. Sanctorum' = CLIII *d*.
>228 'Item ut supra' = CLI *a*.
>229 'In nat. unius Martyris' Nemo militans (2 Tim. ii. 4–10) .... gloria caelesti.
>230 'Item ut supra', CXLVII *b*.

Finally there are the usual three lessons of the Agenda mortuorum CLXXV *a–c*.

(*j*) A heading 'Incipiunt lectiones cotidianis diebus' introduces a set of nine ferial lessons (234–42), differing mostly from the ferial lessons found elsewhere.[a]

The first is 234. Cum adhuc essemus (Rom. v. 6–11) .... in deo per. d. n. J. C.

The next two found a place in the Standard list among the Sundays after Pentecost, but not in this list: they are 235 = CXIX Pent[13]; 236 = CXXIII Pent[16]. (See above, p. 34.)

Two more are here in duplicate; for 237 = 183 = CXXXI, and 238 = 186 = CXXXIV. The four remaining are real additions.
>239 Ne quis vos decipiat (Col. ii. 8–13) .... omnia delicta.
>240 State et tenete (2 Thess. ii. 15–iii. 5) .... patientia Christi.
>241 Dominus mihi adstitit (2 Tim. iv. 17, 18) .... gloria in saecula.
>242 Deus pacis qui eduxit (Heb. xiii. 20, 21) .... in saecula saeculorum.

Superficially this set seems similar to the Unallotted list in We (p. 34), but its nature and contents are far from having the same interest. All the nine, however, are placed in the order of the books from which they are taken; only in that degree they are comparable to We's list of Unallotted epistles.

§ 2. This lectionary differs, then, much from the Standard. Not only is its larger provision for Saints conspicuous, but at the set of Lenten Thursdays, and again in the series for Sundays after Pentecost, it is clear that this is a different type. The arrangement also is different as well as the detail; and, in particular, the alternation of blocks of Sundays and blocks of Festivals through the summer is a characteristic feature. The writer of Alc MS. Paris B.N. Latin 9452 claims in the Preface to his Appendix

---

[a] But 234, 239, and 240 are found see p. 34.

Alcuin's Lectionary

that this lectionary is taken from the genuine Comes[a] as revised and corrected by Alcuin at the direction of Charlemagne: 'Hunc codicem, qui ab ecclesiasticis viris Comes appellatur, tua lector noverit perspicacitas ab eo codice sumptum, quem constat ab Albino eruditissimo viro (Karolo sapientissimo imperatore praecipiente) lima rectitudinis esse politum atque emendatum.' This carefully edited text, the scribe trusts, will be carefully preserved by future transcribers.[b]

Is the claim justified? There is no doubt that Alcuin did some editorial work to the Lectionary, as well as to the Sacramentary. The books at St. Riquier in 831[c] comprised a 'Missalis Gregorianum et Gelasianum modernis temporibus ab Albino ordinatus' (No. 211) and also 'lectionarius plenarius a supradicto Albino ordinatus' (No. 237). The Emperor's own constitution on the correction of the church-books[d] is not so explicit about Alcuin's work on the lectionary of mass as it is about the similar work of Paul the Deacon on the lessons of the Night-office: but there is no reason to doubt that it was done, or that this Scribe was propagating the Alcuinian revision. The surprising thing is (so far as extant evidence goes) that this revision seems to count for so little: and even to stand apart from the main stream as represented by the bulk of the MSS. available, whether called lectionary or Comes.

The Paris MS., however, does not quite stand alone. Dom Morin has described a similar MS. which throws much light on the situation.[e] It shows that the Appendix was subsequently incorporated into the body of the work: thus there was repeated here what happened also in the parallel case of the Sacramentary. Moreover, also, the writer rewrote this preface and relegated it to the end of the enlarged lectionary. Dom Morin gives reasons for thinking that the writer was Helisachar, the Imperial Chancellor, writing some 20–25 years after Alcuin's death. Thus was the Supplementer himself supplemented.

It is not very easy to say exactly what Alcuin's work on the so-called 'Comes' had been. Presumably he had corrected the Vulgate text, since the securing of a correct biblical text was the main objective of the reform of church-books which Charlemagne

---

[a] This term can only be loosely applicable to the MS. See below, p. 77.
[b] See the preface in Tommasi or Ranke. Also in *R.B.* xxix (1912) 341–8.
[c] G. Becker, *Catalogi Bibliothecarum Antiqui* (Bonn, 1885) § 11.
[d] *Mon. Germ. Hist.: Capitularia* (ed. Boretius) i. 80.
[e] See *R.B.* xxix (1912) 341–8. It is a Freising MS. of the early 10th century, now Munich, MS. Clm. 6424.

carried out. But did Alcuin also frame this particular form of lectionary? He wrote a short poem[a] by way of Preface 'Ad Librum Comitem': but this does not reveal much, except that the list both began and ended with Christmas. This point is important because it shows that the so-called 'Comes' of Alcuin differed from the Comes of Pseudo-Jerome which is to be described shortly, among the descendants of the Standard Epistle-list: thus, again, the isolation of Alc from the main stream of tradition comes into view.

It is not surprising, then, that Helisachar should be dissatisfied with the contents of the Alcuinian lectionary and should add an Appendix of his own. His explanations as given in his Preface are, however, not very clear. He includes lessons which had been in use, but had been omitted (he says) by Alcuin for the sake of conformity to the Gregorian Sacramentary.[b] He mentions specially lessons for Easter Even, for ferias, and some other ecclesiastical offices.

In fact, of the 65 epistles added in the Appendix,[c] Nos. 1–8 are restored lessons from the Temporale of the Standard list, including Easter Even. Nos. 52, 53 are similarly restored from the Commune, and Nos. 56–65 from the Votive Section. A group of eight (9–16) supply epistles for the Wednesdays after Easter (see p. 56). In the middle of them there is a displaced Saints-day restored, the Invention of the Cross (No. LXXX and AA 13).

At first sight it is difficult to determine the reason for other entries, because from AA 18 to AA 49 no rubric is given; but Helisachar's own method and motive is thus clearly explained. But he misstates Alcuin's: for, in fact, Alc does not agree with the Hadrianum, nor with the Appendix to it, which is supposed to be Alcuinian, in the details of Easter Even, nor in the disposition of Sundays, nor in the general method.

NOTE

The whole Appendix runs thus:
1 = IV a; 2 = III a; 3 = VIII; 4 = XXV; 5–8 = LXVI* b, c, g, h.
9 Obedite (Heb. xiii. 17–21) .... gloria in s. saec. Oct Pasch[1] iv.

[a] See *Mon. Germ. Hist.* (*Poetæ*, vol. i. 219).

[b] 'Quas praedictus vir peritissimus, imitando ac sequendo libellum papae Gregorii sacramentorum, omisit.'

[c] A comparison with Bob, p. 73, shows that these represent a set of Wednesdays and Fridays after Pentecost, allowing for some which S used for Sundays 3, 6, 10, 17, 4 after Pentecost, and the Compiler of Bob therefore did not use for this purpose. The rest of the entries from 50 onwards have their rubrics, and they corroborate the explanation here given.

Alcuin's Lectionary 47

10 Scientes quod (1 Pet. i. 18–25) .... in aeternum. Oct Pasch²iv.
11 Haec scribo (1 Jo. ii. 1–8) .... lucet. Oct Pasch³iv.
12 Omnes vos (1 Thess. v. 5–11) .... facitis in .... Oct Pasch⁴iv.
13 = LXXX Invention of the Cross.
14 *Estote* = LXXXV for Asc¹; A 137 for Pent³; here for Asc¹iv.
15 Videmus J. (Heb. ii. 9–iii. 1) .... confessionis n. Asc¹vi.
16 has the rubric 'Lectiones inf. ebd. post Oct Pasch'.
   From 17–49 there is no direction given but 'Item alia'.
16 Christus resurrexit (1 Cor. xv. 20–3) .... ordine. Oct Pasch¹.
17 Mortificate (Col. iii. 5–11) .... in omnibus Christus. Oct Pent¹iv in Fi.
18 *Nolite mirari* = XCVI for Pent³.
19 Omne quodcunque (Col. iii. 17–24) .... hereditatis. Oct Pent³iv in Fi. Pent⁸vi in Bob.
20 Habemus gratiam (Heb. xii. 28–xiii. 8) .... hodie et in s. s. Pent⁷iv. Pent⁹iv.
21 *Omnes unianimes* = CIII for Pent⁶.
22 *Non simus* = CXII for Pent¹⁰.
23 Nescitis quoniam cui (Rom. vi. 16–18) .... iustitiae. Pent¹²iv. Pent⁹vi.
24 Non praedicamus nos (2 Cor. iv. 5–10) .... manifestetur. Pent¹³iv. Pent¹⁰vi.
25 Gratias agentes (Col. i. 12–18) .... primatum tenens. Pent¹⁶iv. Pent¹¹vi.
26 *Obsecro vos* = CXXIV for Pent¹⁷.
27 Denuntiamus (2 Thess. iii. 6–13) .... bene facientes. Pent²¹iv. Pent¹⁵iv.
28 Finis praecepti (1 Tim. i. 5–12) .... confortauit. Pent²³iv. Pent¹⁵vi.
29 Nolo vos ignorare (Rom. xi. 25–36) .... Ipsi gloria in s. saec. Pent²⁵iv. Pent¹⁶vi.
30 Nemo nostrum (Rom. xiv. 7–12) .... reddet deo. Pent¹⁷iv.
31 Succincti lumbos (1 Pet. i. 13–16) .... sanctus sum. Pent¹⁷vi.
32 Viuus est sermo (Heb. iv. 12–16) .... opportuno. Pent¹⁷vii.
33 Quicunque totam (James ii. 10–13) .... iudicio. Pent¹⁹iv.
34 Non regnet (Rom. vi. 12–14) .... gratia. Pent¹⁹vi.
35 Haec scribo (1 John i. 4–9) .... iniquitate. Pent¹⁹vii.
36 *Humiliamini* = XCIX for Pent⁴.
37 Videte vocationem (1 Cor. i. 26–31) .... glorietur. Pent²⁰iv.
38 Subditi estote (James iv. 7–12) .... liberare. Pent²⁰vi.
39 Nunc filii dei (1 John iii. 2–9) .... natus est. Pent²⁰vii.
40 Habentes fiduciam (Heb. x. 19–31) .... dei uiui. Pent²¹iv.
41 Hoc non lateat (2 Pet. iii. 8–14) .... in pace. Pent²¹vi.
42 Scimus quoniam (Rom. iii. 19–24) .... quod est in C. J. d. n. Pent²¹vii.
43 Quod si zelum (James iii. 14–18) .... pacem. Pent²²iv.
44 Si cor non (1 John iii. 21–4) .... in eo. Pent²²vi.
45 De caritate (1 Thess. iv. 9–12) .... desideretis. Pent²³iv.
46 Nouit dominus (2 Tim. ii. 19–21) .... paratum. Pent²³vi.

47 Exerce teipsum (1 Tim. iv. 7–10) . . . . fidelium. Pent²⁴iv.
48 Omnis disciplina (Heb. xii. 11–14) . . . . videbit d. Pent²⁴vi.
49 Videte ne forte (Heb. iii. 12–14) . . . . retineamus. Nat⁻⁵iv.
50 *Gratias agere* = CLI *h* for Nat⁻⁵iv. Nat⁻⁴iv.
51 Patientes estote (James v. 7–10) . . . . in nomine d. Nat⁻³vi.
52 *Benedictio d.* = CXXXVII ⎫
53 *Testificor* = CXLIX   ⎭ for Apost. Mr. or Conf.
54 Scimus quod lex (Rom. vii. 14–25) . . . . gratia dei. 'Pro se ipso.'
55 Rectorem te (Ecclus. composite) . . . . gratiam. Votive, for the King.
56 = CLXXIII. 57, 58 = CLXXII *a, b*. 59 = CLXXIV.
60 = CLIX *b*. 61 = CLX. 62 = CLXI *b*.
63 = CLXI *a* 'ad regem benedicendum'. 64 = CLXXI.
65 = CLXX.
Added later for St. Luke's day Si voluntas (2 Cor. viii. 12–21).

CHAPTER IV

Development

WE turn now to consider the development of the Standard series, remembering that, although there is no MS. available which exhibits it exactly, it is easily discoverable through considering the enumeration which is given in the Corbie MS. (pp. 1–24). This numbering is not quite regular;[a] but it is sufficiently so to make clear the difference between the entries of the series, as numbered, and the entries subsequently made to it, which bear no number in the enumeration. They are as follows:

St. James. July 25. The Lesson is in the Commune as CLI *d*.

St. Bartholomew.	Aug. 24.	CXLVII *a*.
Nativity of the B.V.M.	Sept. 8.	CXVIII.
Exalt. of the Cross.	Sept. 14.	LXI.
St. Matthew.	Sept. 21 with a Vigil.	CLIV & CXLVII *e*.
SS. Simon & Jude.	Oct. 28 with a Vigil.	CLIII *a* & CXLVIII *c*.

Thus it is clear that no fresh lessons have been brought in, but only fresh Holy-days, to the number of six, four of them being days of Apostles. This later insertion of the feasts of Apostles has

---

[a] There is no number prefixed at Easter Even to the lessons of the Vigil; but this is not the case with the Vigil of Pentecost. The Number XCVIII, which should stand before the lessons of Saturday in the Summer Embertide, is lacking; though this is not the case in the other Embertides: and the omission is therefore due to an original piece of carelessness. The Number CXVIII is lacking in the list itself, but it is given in the preliminary list of liturgical days (p. 27).

Development

already been noted as being characteristic of the Gospel-lists: and the same is true of the two other entries.[a]

The other MSS., those, that is, which have been used here as available for comparison with the Standard, are few in number as compared with the wealth of Gospel-Books. The Epistle-Books, as a class, had not the glamour belonging to the Gospel-Books proper, containing the whole of the Four Gospels; nor even the derived glamour which belonged to the Books containing the Series of Liturgical Gospels. Later on, with the rise of 'Missale plenum', they became of no practical value. Consequently, while Gospel-Books, for the magnificence of their execution and their binding, were preserved, either as Treasures or as containing valuable documents recorded in them, the MSS. containing the list, or even the full text, of the other Mass-lessons were of no such account, and tended to disappear. Only a few have been preserved, either because they were exceptionally fine MSS., or else by some chance.

II

Those that have been utilized for the purposes of this study fall into four classes:

(*a*) Lists which merely give the incipit and explicit of each lesson used 'for the Epistle'.
(*b*) MSS. which contain such lessons in full.
(*c*) Lists which represent the 'Comes' entries, *i.e.* those associating the Epistle-list and the Gospel-list together, but not giving the lessons in full.
(*d*) The 'Comes', in its complete form, giving both Epistles and Gospels in full.[b]

The only representative of (*a*)—a mere list—is We; a brief MS. containing an Epistle-list, and a separate Gospel-list. It has been already described (vol. II, p. 74, and above, p. 27).

In (*b*) fall the Epistle-books proper, which are books intended for liturgical use, and contain all the lessons, other than the Gospels, in full. Eight of these are taken into account here.

1. Corbie. The Corbie MS., which is the numbered Standard series, in the purest form available, but containing a few unnumbered entries inserted into the text. This MS. has already been described with its further additions (p. 25).

---
[a] See vol. I, pp. 66, 78, 120 &c., 133.
[b] In a Capuan deed of Exchange dated 1065, a distinction is drawn in the list of Church books between 'liber comite maiore unum' and 'minori duo'. Gattula, *Hist. Abb. Cassin.* (Venice, 1733) i, p. 254.

2. Fi, which follows the Standard series with some differences and additions.
3. Mz, which has another form of the Standard series.
4. Val, which is a much enlarged form of it.
5. TP, a late form of it.
6. Bes, the same.
7. C, an early form, and Italian with some variants; but it is only partly preserved.

Besides 8. Alc, the early Epistle-book described above (pp. 40–48) which differs markedly from the Standard, and forms a separate type.

(c) Mu. The list of a Comes, is represented only by the Murbach MS., which seems to have been made to fit a 'Mixed Sacramentary'.

(d) The Comes proper is represented by a dozen or so of MSS.
1. Pal. Similar to the Standard series, so far as Epistles are concerned, but with some marked differences.
2. Aud. A fine and early Comes, at Chartres.
3. Qt. A fine Comes, comparable with the Standard series, but showing signs of a different scheme of numbering the items.
4. Ver. An incomplete Comes, similar to the Standard, but with a restricted Sanctorale. It has traces of a different scheme of numbering.
5. Qf. A fine MS., probably from Trier.
6. Pam. The Comes, summarized by Pamelius.
7. Bob. A Comes recast to suit a Sacramentary like the 'Hadrianum'.
8. Theo. The Comes Theotinchi, printed by Baluze. It is a great enlargement of the Standard scheme with lessons added for a daily Mass. It is handled separately in Chapter VIII.
9. Bml. A late German Comes, which has the Sanctorale set apart from the Temporale, as in the later Books of the Gospels.
10. MS. A late German Comes (not so called) containing the Epistles and Gospels, also set in blocks.
11. TQ. A late MS., which does not include any Epistles after Epiph[5].

These MSS. are more fully described at the end of this chapter (pp. 67–73).

In tracing the development of the Epistle-list through the ninth and tenth centuries the greater part of these four groups of

Temporale

MSS. can be taken together—those called 'lectionary' as well as those called 'Comes'.[a] But the time will come when it is no longer possible to defer the question as to the origin and nature of the Comes itself. Our survey of the development can be made jointly over the whole area covered by the Temporale, the Commune, and the collection of Votive masses: but when the survey of the Sanctorale is reached, it will be desirable to treat the lectionaries separately from the Comes MSS.; and indeed these themselves will break up into two sections.

III

We begin, then, the survey of the development with the Temporale, which naturally takes the first place.

In the survey of the Temporale, five sections (1–5) will suffice to describe the divergences from S. in the ordinary year: then § 6 deals with the addition to S. of Epistles for Wednesdays, and § 7 with the additions for Fridays. § 8 deals with the Commune and § 9 with the Votives. With § 10 the Sanctorale is reached: but the survey of development there is at present confined to the Lectionaries, while the rest of that survey is deferred till the history of the Comes itself has been considered.

§ 1. In the development of the Temporale up to Lent the following points are to be noted.

(*a*) There is variety in the order of the lessons for the four Masses of Christmas Day: all the eight lessons are given, but Qf and Val, which begin with Advent, have I *a* in a different position. For St. John's Day some give an Epistle as well as the lesson; Corbie does so (VI *a*) and the greater number of the rest: but many omit it. We (the Earlier Series) had it here, and added *Justum deduxit* CLI *d* as well.

(*b*) Nativ¹ is absent in Val perhaps only by mistake. Bob has instead *Considerate*, Alc 17: and it keeps IX for Nativ².

(*c*) Oct Nativ. exhibits variety. Commonly in place of VIII *Audistis* either II, II *a*, or III is repeated from Christmas: but there are other alternatives.

    Priusquam (Gal. iii. 23–iv. 2) . . . . a patre. in Mz, Pal, Pam.
    Ne quis uos (Col. ii. 8–13) . . . . delicta. in Bob, with II also.
    Gaudete in d. (Phil. iii. 1–8) . . . . scientiam d. n. in Mu, & Qt.
    Arbitramur iustificari (Rom. iii. 28–iv. 12) . . . . Abrahae. in
        Bes, with II *a*.

The divergence shows the lateness of any such entry.

[a] Except Alc, which has been already handled (Chapter III); and Theo, which comes later (see Chapter VIII).

(*d*) Vig Epiph is like Oct Nativ in that III, a Christmas Epistle, is repeated usually; but Pal, Pam, Fi, Mz, like Corbie, have x. Similar divergence prevails at the octave. In many, as in We, there is no such day given; most of the rest agree with Corbie in prescribing XIII, but Qt has *Fidelis sermo* Alc16; and Val repeats Epiph x. The Sundays following are mostly uniform: but Mz and Val omit *Obsecro* XII. Corbie, representing S, and others end the series with Theoph[4] XVI *Nemini q.*, but the larger number provide variously for a fifth Sunday, Theoph[5]. It is usually Induite vos (Col. iii. 12–17) .... deo et patri: but Val repeats VIII here, keeping Induite for Epiph[6], and Bob (like Alc) has Noli erubescere (2 Tim. i. 8–13) A. 20 .... et dilectione in J.C. d. n. The addition of new lessons for week-days previous to Lent is explained later on.

§ 2 (*a*). In Lent, the variants come at the familiar points—the Thursdays and the two familiar Saturdays L vii and XL[5]vii, which are days added later. The Standard series for the Thursdays prevails generally, though there is some inversion of order in the third and fourth weeks: but Aud, Qf, and Bob, like Alc, draw upon a rival series, which is only partly the same, and is as follows:

XL[1]v. Orauit Esdras (Neh. i. 5–11) A. 39.
XL[2]v. *Misericordiae* (Thren. iii. 22 &c.) CLXV *b*.
XL[3]v. *Beatus vir* (Jer. xvii. 7–10). A. 57.
XL[4]v. *Helisaeus* (4 Reg. xiii. 14–21) A. 64.
XL[5]v. *Verbum quod* (Jer. vii. 1–7) XLIV and A 73.

At L v all agree with S if they make provision at all: but Aud, Qt, Bob make none.

At XL[5]vii two MSS. (Qf and Bob) have *Exalta satis* (Zach. ix. 9–16) A 75 instead of *Dixerunt impii* LX: while Aud has LXIII *Domine demonstrasti* instead, and Val adds Nos debemus (2 Thess. ii. 13, 14) .... in adquisitionem gloriae d. n. J. Christi, as well.

As a rule the duplicate Lenten lessons following XXIX, L, LIII, LXII, LXIII, LXIV, LXVI are preserved in all the lists, but sometimes one or another is omitted.

(*b*) The next points that call for attention are the Vigil lessons at Easter Even and Whitsun Eve.

At Easter Even the full set of Twelve Lessons (with or without four Canticles) is given in S, Fi, Mu, Bob, and in Pam, C, and Ver with some slight difference; for Pam has for the fifth *Omnes sitientes* (LIII *a*); and Ver has for the sixth Exultate in laetitia (Jer. xxxi. 7–14) .... adimplebitur: while C has Surgite, i.e. the same passage but beginning at verse 6. Mz has only eleven,

Embertide

omitting the twelfth; and Bes has nine, namely *acbd(e)*; *fghj*; *m(o)* (following the letters as shown at p. 9).

Pal has *abcde*; *Omnes sitientes* (LIII *a*) *ghjk l–o*.

Val originally had only seven—*abdc nmj*; but later, marginally, the number was made up to twelve.

Qt has only the first five and Qf a different five:—*adjmf*.

There are only four in Aud and TP, viz.—*adjf*.

This variety of usage is paralleled in the different Sacramentaries: for example, the full set of twelve lessons is given in the Appendix to the Hadrianum, in the mixed Sacramentaries called RS,[a] and in the Rossianum.[b] The Vatican Gelasian has ten, omitting *g* and *m*. Hadrian and Padua have the same four as Aud and TP; in the Ordo Romanus I (Appendix) there is a different set of four—*adjm*; but Ordo Romanus X prescribes the whole twelve, to be read in Latin first and then in Greek.[c]

The similar situation at Whitsun Eve is also varied. No lessons are given at all in Fi, Qt. Apart from the canticles, S, Mu, Pam, Ver have seven of the Easter lessons—*acdnjgp*, thus agreeing with the Gelasian Sacramentary, V, and the Appendix to the Hadrianum, and the Mixed Sacramentary Ross. Yet Pal has only the first four of these—*acdm*. Another group figures in the Sacramentaries of Hadrian and Padua—*cmjgp*; and this set of five seems to be the source of sets given in these lectionaries; for Qf, Bob have *cmjg*: Val has a different set of five—*cn* with Gaudens gaudebo (Hab. iii. 18, 19) . . . . virtus mea, and *jg*; while elsewhere there are only three, viz. in TP only *cmj*, and in Aud only *cmg*. Thus the Vigil lessons are marked by great variety.

§ 3. The four Embertides may be conveniently considered together; and they exhibit little variation. At XL² the entry 'Vacat' has been preserved in some lists—Fi, Mz.

At the summer Embertide there is considerable variation as to the equating of the Fast-days with the Pentecostal Season. The Standard list sets them after Pent[3]; and this is the most usual position. It is at this date rare to find them set according to modern custom, in Whitsun Week; but TP adds them there. Some prefer the next week, as Val and Bob, Theo, *i.e.* after Pent[1]. There is none that chooses the week following Pent[2]: but Aud. Qt, Qf, Ver go as late as the week after Pent[4].

There is less variation as to the position in September; the Fast days follow No. cxxv in the Standard, and elsewhere: and with them goes the corresponding Sunday, whether it be called

---

[a] Vol. I, p. 52.   [b] Ed. J. Brinktrine (Freiburg, 1930).
[c] *P. L.* lxxviii, 955, 1014.

'Dominica mensis Septembris' or by some other enumeration or title.

In Advent the usual position of Embertide is in the third week: but Aud, Qt, Ver, and Bob place the Fast-days in the fourth week.

§ 4. Litania maior precedes Ascension,[a] usually having LXXXII alone: but Aud adds *Obsecro vos* from CLXIX: Bes adds the succeeding verses *alio modo* Volo ergo viros (1 Tim. ii. 8–15) .... sobrietate. Val gives three lessons 'In tribus letaniis': *Humiliamini* from XCIX, *Omnes unanimes* from CIII, and *Facite iudicium* (Jer. xxii. 3, 4) A 221. C agrees, but has CXLVIII *b Unicuique* for the third.

§ 5. There is some variation in the Sundays after Pentecost: but, just as after the Epiphany there is no marked variation in the Epistle-lists to be noted as regards Sundays such as there was in the Gospel-lists, so the same is the case after Pentecost also. There is no more trace of the older tradition which provided for only twenty Sundays between Pentecost and Advent, except perhaps in C. The Standard list provides for full twenty-five Sundays. This is the usual number, though the nomenclature varies. The commonest is Pent$^{1-25}$ with a fifth Sunday before Christmas as No. CXXXIX: but this is called Oct Pent^{25} in Mu and Qf; and Pent^{26} in Bes. The Roman method of reckoning the later Sundays in groups—after the Apostles, after St. Lawrence, and after Michaelmas, is adopted in Val, Aud, Qt, Ver, and Theo; while Val calls CXXIX the Sunday after St. Cyprian, placing it between those reckoned from St. Lawrence and those reckoned from Michaelmas. The Comes in several cases (Aud, Qt, Ver, and Theo) reckons CXXV as the Sunday before Embertide and CXXIX as the Sunday after it, where Val has a Lawr^6 and its single Sunday after St. Cyprian: so Ang^1 always begins with CXXXI: but Theo is exceptional in calling these two Sundays 'Dom. Mensis sexti', following them up with a 'Dom. mensis septimi' and then Cypr^3.

Two of C's Epistles are not in S but are in Alc. The rest are as in S, but shifted two places or one place earlier. They differ more in order from Alc. The scribe seems to have been alive to C's peculiarity, for he took hereabouts the precaution of adding a cue for the Gospel. These Gospel cues are shown in the table by their symbols (see vol. II, p. 114); and the regularity from T^6 onwards, as contrasted with the earlier part, suggests a usage which had not yet adopted more than two of the Sundays added in July. For this subject see vol. II, Index under 'Summer Sundays'.

[a] After Oct Pasch^3 in Bob.

Summer Sundays

C is not only peculiar at this point but tantalizingly incomplete. Pent is lacking and the weeks following up to Pent³. The disposition of its Sundays ensuing, so far as they exist, is best shown in tabular form:—two columns for the Epistle and one for the Gospel.

C. Pent⁴ Sicut per unius   Alc 148 (Apost¹)   T³
   Pent⁵ = cviii (Pent⁷) Alc 149 (Apost²)   T²
   Pent⁶ = cx (Pent⁸)   Alc 150 (Apost³)   T⁶
   Pent⁷ = cxi (Pent⁹)   Alc 152 (Apost⁵)   T⁷
   Pent⁸ = cxii (Pent¹⁰)   AA 82   T⁸
   Pent⁹ = cxiii (Pent¹¹) A 126 (Oct Pent)   T⁹
   Pent¹⁰ = cxv (Pent¹²)   T¹⁰ᵃ
   Pent¹¹ = cxix (Pent¹³) A 235 (Quotid)   T¹¹
   Pent¹² Scimus quoniam   A 163 (Lawr²)   T¹²
   Pent¹³ = cxxi (Pent¹⁴) A 165 (Lawr⁴)   T¹³
   Pent¹⁴ = cxxii (Pent¹⁵) A 166 (Lawr⁵)

There are, further, two lists which depart considerably from this normal Trinity-tide, in contents as well as in arrangement and nomenclature of the Sundays—the Epistle-list Val, and the Comes Aud.

Val puts No. c on the Sunday marked 'Vacat' following Pent¹. It then has Pent² Cum adhuc (Rom. v. 6–11) A 234 .... in deo, instead of xcv, and Pent³ *Sicut per unius* (Rom. v. 18–21) A 148 (p. 42) instead of xcvi. Then xciv, c, ciii are omitted and cviii is used for Pent⁴.

The series Apost¹⁻⁵ follows, and cxix was perhaps originally called Apost⁶; but the enumeration has been altered, and it stands now as Pent⁶.

For Lawr¹ is inserted *Scimus quoniam* A 163 (p. 42). Then follow Lawr²⁻⁶ = Nos. cxxi–cxxv; and when we reach cxxix, it (as already noted) is called the Sunday after St. Cyprian. Then appear nine Sundays after 'Angeli', being the rest of the usual series down to cxxxix with two additions made from a list like that of the unallotted epistles in We (p. 33), namely Ang⁷ Mortificate (Col. iii. 5–11) AA 17 (p. 47), and Ang⁸ Induite vos. (Col. iii. 12–17) ... deo et patri: thus making twenty-seven in all.[a]

In Aud, after Oct Pent³ comes Embertide, with No. c at the Sunday following, called 'Dominica ut supra'. The next Sunday is called 'Dom. ante Natale Apostolorum', and instead of ciii it has *Sicut per unius* A 148. Then follows Dom. post Natale Apostolorum (cviii) and thereafter cx, cxi, cxii are reckoned as 'post Oct Apostolorum'. Here a Sunday is interpolated as Oct Apost⁴ and given the Epistle *Non omnis caro* (1 Cor. xv. 39–46) A 162, which is usually found in the week following. Thus cxiii, cxiv become Oct Apost⁵,⁶.

The five Sundays following St. Lawrence are normal, and after them come the two connected with Embertide, 'Dom. mensis septimi' cxxv, and 'Dom.

---

[a] See the supplemental list and table above, p. 34.

unde supra' cxxix. After Ang³, cxxxiv is omitted, so that cxxxv and cxxxvi become Ang⁴,⁵. Then come three additions by way of compensation; Angeli⁶ Gratias agimus deo (Col. i. 12–18) AA 25.

Ang⁷ *Mortificate* as in Val above, but the passage is not, as there, continued to form the Epistle for Ang⁸.

Here instead is Ang⁸, Memores enim (1 Thess. ii. 9–13) .... credidistis in ipso; which also is one of We's supplemental list.

Only one other small variant remains yet to be recorded: At Pent²⁵ Mz has an insertion Nolo enim vos ignorare (Rom. xi. 25–36) AA 29 .... and then comes cxxxix as Nativ⁻⁵.

§ 6. We pass on now from the variants of the Temporale of S to consider additions for week-days. The earliest Epistle-lists make no provision for ordinary week-days, differing in this respect from the earlier Gospel-lists. Not only We, but the Standard series also, has none: and the same is true of Val and Aud as well as of the Alcuinian series, in the earlier part of the year down to Lent. But in the rest provision begins to be made at least for Wednesdays.

(*a*) The provision for Wednesdays in the weeks after Epiphany is normally as follows, *i.e.* in Fi, Mz, Pal, Mu, Pam:

Theoph¹ iv. *Scimus quoniam* = x.
Theoph² iv. *Audistis dispensationem* = viii.
Theoph³ iv. *Fidelis sermo* A 16 (p. 40).
Theoph⁴ iv. *Sicut per unius* A 148 (p. 42).
Theoph⁵ iv. Videte vocationem AA 37 (p. 47).

In Pal there is also found an epistle for Theoph iv. *Considerate apostolum* (Heb. iii. 1–6) A 17 (p. 40).

The Wednesdays in Septuagesima and Sexagesima are thus given in Fi, Mz, Mu, Pam,[a] and as an afterthought in Val.

LXX. iv. Festinemus ingredi (Heb. iv. 11–16) (*cp.* AA 32, p. 47).

LX. iv. Recogitate (Heb. xii. 3–9) .... et viuemus,
but these are thus rarer than those after Epiphany.

(*b*) In Eastertide the provision for Wednesdays is also in Fi, Mz, Pal, Pam; this set is expressly appointed in Alc Appendix, 9–12 and 15 (see p. 46).

Pasch¹ iv. Obedite praepositis (Heb. xiii. 17–21).
Oct Pasch¹ iv. Scientes quod non (1 Pet. i. 18–25).
Oct Pasch² iv. Haec scribo ut (1 Jo. ii. 1–8).
Oct Pasch³ iv. Omnes vos filii (1 Thess. v. 5–11).
Asc¹ iv. Vidimus J. propter[b] (Heb. ii. 9–iii. 1).

[a] These also are on We's Unallotted list (p. 34).

[b] Fi repeats lxxxiii for Asc¹ vi; and Mz has it here, having had cxxv *Unicuique nostrum* in place of it at Vig Asc.

Wednesdays

Val has only Oct Pasch³. iv. *Nolite mirari* = xcvi; which is repeated again at Vig Asc in place of lxxxiii.

§ 7. In the summer the following are those provided for the Wednesdays in Fi: but note that the mode of reckoning the Sundays changes after the first four.

Oct Pent iv. Si Christus praedicatur (1 Cor. xv. 12–23) . . . . in suo ordine.

Oct Pent¹ iv. Mortificate (Col. iii. 5–11) AA 17 . . . . in omnibus Christus . . . .

Oct Pent² iv. xcvii and xcvii *a* (Ember week).

Oct Pent³ iv. Omne quodcunque facitis (Col. iii. 17–24) AA 19 . . . . haereditatis per . . . .

Pent⁵ iv. Non cesso gratias (Ephes. i. 16–21) A 101 . . . . quod nominatur in saec. saec.

Pent⁶ iv. *Obsecro primum omnium* (1 Tim. ii. 1–7) = clxix.

Pent⁷ iv. Habemus gratiam per quam (Heb. xii. 28–xiii. 8) AA 20 . . . . heri et hodie. Ipse . . . .

Pent⁸ iv. *Nihil damnationis* (Rom. viii 1–6) A 151 (p. 42).

Pent⁹ iv. Quoniam cum adhuc (Rom. v. 6–11) A 234 (p. 44).

Pent¹⁰ iv. Nescitis quoniam cui exhibetis (Rom. vi. 16–18) AA 23 . . . . iustitiae in . . . .

Pent¹¹ iv. Non omnis caro eadem (1 Cor. xv. 39–46) A 162.

Pent¹² iv. *Nescitis quoniam corpora* (1 Cor. vi. 15–20) = clxii.

Pent¹³ iv. Non enim nosmet ipsos (2 Cor. iv. 5–10) . . . . manifestetur.

Pent¹⁴ iv. Scimus q. si terrestris (2 Cor. v. 1–11) A 163 (p. 42).

Pent 15 iv. Nolite iugum ducere (2 Cor. vi. 14–vii. 1) A 164.

Pent¹⁶ iv. Gratias agentes D. Patri (Col. 1. 12–18) AA 25 . . . . primatum tenens.

Pent¹⁷ iv. Videte ne quis (Col. ii. 8–13) A 239.

Pent¹⁸ iv. cxxvi and cxxvi *a* (Ember week). Dom. vacat.

Pent²⁰ iv. State et tenete (2 Thess. ii. 15–iii. 5) A 240.

Pent²¹ iv. Denuntiamus autem v. (2 Thess. iii. 6–13) AA 27 . . . . bene facientes.

Pent²² iv. Nihil intulimus (1 Tim. vi. 7–14) . . . . usque ad adventum DNJC.

Pent²³ iv. Finis autem praecepti (1 Tim. i. 5–12) AA 28 . . . . confortauit.

Pent²⁴ iv. Noli erubescere (2 Tim. i. 8–13) A 20 (p. 40).

Pent²⁵ iv. Nolo vos ignorare (Rom. xi. 25–36) AA 29 . . . . sunt omnia. Ipsi gloria in s.s.

Nativ⁻⁵ iv. Gratias agimus Deo (1 Thess. 1. 2–6) .... cum gaudio s.s.

This table, which is taken from Fi, holds good also for the Wednesdays after Pentecost in the following Epistle-books Mz, TP, Bes, and the following Comes-books Pal, Mu, Pam, but with a few exceptions, besides the differences caused by the variation of the Ember-week after Whitsunday.

(i) Mz differs after Pent[24] iv. The next Sunday (called Oct Pent[24]) takes cxxxvi with *Obedite* (from Pasch[4] iv) for the following Wednesday. Then there is an additional Sunday (called Oct Pent[25]) which takes *Nolo vos ignorare* from the preceding Wednesday, and for the ensuing Wednesday it supplies Os nostrum patet (2 Cor. vi. 11–vii. 1) .... dei vivi.

(ii) In Tp and Bes *Dominica vacat* is supplied with a Wednesday: in TP it is *Os nostrum patet*; and in Bes it is Satagite ut per (2 Pet. i. 10–14) .... signauit mihi.

(iii) Bes also differs in having at Pent[23] iv *Obsecro primum* = CLXIX, and adding a Pent[26] iv Gratias agere debemus (Col. i. 3–11) .... cum gaudio.

(iv) Among the Comes-books the exceptions are that Pal and Pam repeat at Pent[18] iv *Nescitis quoniam* CLXII and omit Pent[25] iv.

(v) Mu varies having at Pent[5] iv *Induite* (Col. iii. 12–17): at Pent[8] iv none: at Pent[19] iv *Mortificate* again: at Pent[22] iv *Obsecro primum*, and yet again for the week following.

§ 8. At a later stage provision was made also for Fridays. This did not affect the Comes-books such as we have before us (except Bob, which, in regard to week-day Epistles, is to be treated separately), but only the Epistle-books under consideration. These received additions for Fridays in all parts of the year, except from Lent to the end of Easter-week and throughout Whitsun-week, where no further provision was needed.

The MSS. that come now into consideration as providing for Fridays are therefore only three, Val, TP, and Bes; but Val only to a small extent to be described separately. Both TP and Bes for the Wednesdays use the series already set out (p. 57), and as regards Fridays TP and Bes agree almost exactly, except where a difference is recorded in the table following.

TP and Bes

Theoph[1] vi. Nolite deficere (2 Thess. iii. 13–16).
Theoph[2] vi. Fidelis sermo ... in hoc (1 Tim. iv. 9–16).
Theoph[3] vi. Bonum est homini (1 Cor. vii. 1–9).
Theoph[4] vi. Orationi instate (Col. iv. 2–6).
Theoph[5] vi. De caritate (1 Thess. iv. 9–12 and v. 28).
LXX. vi. Eramus natura (Eph. ii. 3–7).
LX. vi. Nos sumus desolati (1 Thess. ii. 17–20).

Fridays

Pasch¹ vi. Divitibus (1 Tim. vi. 17–21).
Oct Pasch¹ vi. Certus sum (Rom. xv. 14–17).
Oct Pasch² vi. Dico vobis ut nemo (Col. ii. 4–7).
Oct Pasch³ vi. De temporibus (1 Thess. v. 1–5).
Asc¹ vi. Unusquisque in qua (1 Cor. vii. 20–4).

Oct Pent vi. Dico vobis reuelabitur (2 Thess. ii. 8–14).
Oct Pent¹ vi. Abraham credidit (Gal. iii. 6–11).
Oct Pent²   xcviii (Ember-week).
Oct Pent³ vi. Nolite in personarum (Jac. ii. 1–9).
Oct Pent⁴ vi. Commonere vos (Jude i. 5–13).
Oct Pent⁵ vi. Quid proderit si (Jac. ii. 14–17).
Oct Pent⁶ vi. Si zelum amarum (Jac. iii. 14–18).
Oct Pent⁷ vi. Subditi estote (Jac. iv. 7–10). AA 38.
Oct Pent⁸ vi. Videte ne forte (Heb. iii. 12–14) AA 49.
Oct Pent ⁹ vi. Nolite peregrinari (1 Pet. iv. 12–14).
Oct Pent¹⁰ vi. Cum essetis aliquando (Col. i. 21–3).
Oct Pent¹¹ vi. Cum liber essem (1 Cor. ix. 19–22).
Oct Pent¹² vi. Fugite ab idolorum (1 Cor. x. 14–17).
Oct Pent¹³ vi. Quam gratiarum (1 Thess. iii. 9–13).
Oct Pent¹⁴ vi. Presbyteri qui bene (1 Tim. v. 17–21).
Oct Pent¹⁵ vi. Considerate apostolum (Heb. iii. 1–6). A. 17.
Oct Pent¹⁶ vi. Si qua consolatio (Phil. ii. 1–5).
Oct Pent¹⁷ vi. cxxvii (Ember-week).
Oct Pent¹⁸ (Vacat) vi. Nescitis quoniam iniqui (1 Cor. vi. 9–11).[a]
Oct Pent¹⁹ vi. Omnis qui credit (1 Jo. v. 1–4).
Oct Pent²⁰ vi. Scimus quia omnis (1 Jo. v. 18–20).
Oct Pent²¹ vi. Regnauit mors (Rom. v. 14–17).
Oct Pent ²² vi. Dico igitur et testificor (Eph. iv. 17–20).
Oct Pent²³ vi. Probate quid sit (Eph. v. 10–14).
Oct Pent²⁴ vi. Infirmum in fide (Rom. xiv. 1–6).
Oct Pent²⁵ vi. Habentes itaque (Heb. x. 19–25) AA 40.

Thus the provision for Fridays also is fairly stable.

§ 9. The situation in Advent as regards Wednesdays and Fridays is simple and can be stated all at once.

Adv¹ iv. Patientes estote (Jac. v. 7–10) AA 51 (p. 48).

Adv¹ vi. Loquere que decent (Tit. ii. 1–10) . . . . omnibus TP, Bes.

Adv² iv. Ecce ego mitto (Malachi compound A 25) is used generally, but Bes has Ipsi scitis introitum (1 Thess. ii. 1–8) . . . . facti estis.

---

[a] Bes has instead Scienti bonum (Jac. iv. 17–v. 7) . . . . serotinum.

Adv² vi. Nos vero omnes reuelata (2 Cor. iii. 18–iv. 5) . . . . praedicamus, in TP, Bes.

Adv³ Ember-week.

In TP	*In Bes*
Adv⁴ iv. Unum hoc non lateat (2 Pet. iii. 8–14) AA 41.	Nescitis quoniam iniqui (above, p. 59).
Adv⁴ vi. Aspiciebam in visione (Dan. vii. 7, 9, 10, 13, 14), and Scienti bonum (as in the note on p. 59).	Unusquisque in qua (1 Cor. vii. 20–4) (above).

§ 10. Val, which in many respects takes a line of its own and is in a mutilated state in parts, provides very little for these week-days, and very irregularly, viz., apart from Embertide, six for Wednesdays and one for a Friday, as follows:

Apost¹ iv. *Nescitis quoniam cui.*
Lawr¹ iv. Memores estote (Eph. ii. 11–16) . . . . in ipso.
Lawr² iv. *State et tenete.*
Lawr³ iv. *Denuntiamus.*
Lawr⁵ iv. Hoc igitur dico (Eph. iv. 17–24) . . . . veritatis.
Lawr⁶. Ember-week.
Lawr⁴ vi. *Fidelis sermo*, A. 16.

§ 11. There remains still Bob to be described, and separately, because it takes an independent line in providing for week-days, deriving most of its later material from AA, and in a systematic way.

Theoph iv. Noli timere terra (Joel ii. 21–6) A 223 (p. 43).
Theoph vi. *Nolite iugum ducere* A 164.
Theoph² v. *Induite vos sicut* AA 19.
Theoph³ iv. *Audistis dispensationem* = viii.
Theoph³ vi. *Fidelis sermo* A 16.
Theoph⁴ iv. *Omnes vos filii* AA 12.
Theoph⁴ vi. *Confido in vobis* = lxxx.
LXX iv. *State et tenete* A 240.
LXX vi. *Dominus mihi astitit* A 241.
LX iv. *Sicut per unius* A 148.
LX vi. *Deus autem pacis* A 242.
Dom post Albas iv. *Obedite prepositis* = AA 9.
Dom post Albas iv. *Christus resurrexit* AA 16.
Dom post Albas vii. *Cum adhuc essemus* A 234.
Oct Pasch¹ iv. *Scientes quod non* AA 10.
Dom 2 post Albas iv. *Haec scribo ut* AA 11.
Asc vii. *Obsecro igitur primum* clxix (to ver. 6).
Asc¹ iv. *Unicuique autem nostrum* cxlviii *b*.

Oct Pent IV }
Oct Pent VI } Embertide.
Oct Pent VII }
Pent² VI. *Deus qui diues est* A 116.
Pent⁸ IV. *Videmus Jesum* AA 15.
Pent⁸ VI. *Omne quodcumque* AA 19.
From this point onward all comes from AA, down to Advent. Note that AA 18, 21, 22, 26, 36, being used for Sundays, are not used for this purpose.
Pent⁹ IV. *Habemus gratiam* AA 20.
Pent⁹ VI. *Nescitis quoniam cui* AA 23
Pent¹⁰ VI. *Non predicamus nosmet* AA 24.
Pent¹¹ VI. *Gratias agentes* AA 25.
The series ends thus:
Nativ⁻⁵ IV. *Videte ne forte* AA 49.
Nativ⁻⁵ VI. *Nihil nunc damnationis* A 151.
Nativ⁻⁴ IV. *Gratias agere* AA 50.
Nativ⁻³ VI. *Patientes estote* AA 51.
Nativ⁻² IV. *Nolite amittere* A 209.

§ 12. With regard to the Commune Sanctorum the first thing to notice is that there are MSS. which have none. These are Aud, Pam, and Qf, all of them Comes-documents. It is possible therefore that the absence of Commune is due in their case to the assimilation of the Epistle-series, which otherwise has some sort of a Commune, to the method of the Gospel-series which, as we have seen, in its earlier forms as a rule has none. In the case of the other Comes-documents the opposite policy seems to have prevailed; the custom of having a Commune which is prevalent in the Epistle-lists has been preserved, and the Gospel-series has been assimilated to the method of the Epistle-series.

Where a Commune is found, the influence of the Standard Epistle series is usually notable: but our existing authorities differ from it by omission, addition, or alteration. It would seem that at one time no provision was made in the Commune for Apostles. This is natural enough; for until (in the 9–10th century) the great insertion of new festivals of Apostles took place, very few of such days were observed in the Kalendar; and those that were observed were of such a distinctive character that they would naturally have proper epistles, and be placed in the Sanctorale. Fi and Mu in particular are in that position: they begin their Commune with *Vigilia unius sacerdotis*. In Mu the whole of the Epistles in Nos. XLVII and XLVIII are wanting: in Fi all of these

Epistles are used, but they are allotted to individual new feasts of Apostles in the Sanctorale, CXLVII *a* to St. Matthew, CXLVII *b* to St. Thomas, CXLVIII *b* to St. Matthew and CXLVIII *a* and *c* to SS. Simon and Jude.[a]

We are thus pointed back to an earlier stage in the development of the Commune than that exhibited in the Standard series.

A later stage is shown by the additions. Their presence needs no explanation, as it is a natural result of development.

It is only necessary therefore to record them.

Fi adds:

(*a*) 1 Conf. Dilectus deo et hominibus (Ecclus. xlv. 1–6) . . . . disciplinae.

(*b*) Plur. SS. Qui timent d. (Ecclus. ii. 18–21) . . . . ad inspectionem illius.

(*c*)   ,,   Sapientiam omnium ant. (Ecclus. xxxix. 1–5) . . . . temptabit.

(*d*) Virg.   Qui gloriatur in deo XVIII.

(*e*)   ,,   De virginibus (1 Cor. vii. 25–34) . . . . corpore et spiritu.[b]

Mz adds:

(*f*) 1 Sac. Dedit d. confessionem (Ecclus. xlvii. 9–13; xxiv. 1–4) . . . . benedicetur.

(*g*) Virg.   Dominus mihi astitit (2 Tim. iv. 17, 18) A. 241.

This set of additions is much in evidence in the other MSS., though the classification sometimes varies:

(*a*) in TP, Pal, Mu.
(*b*) in Mz, Pal.
(*c*) in Mz, TP, Mu.
(*d*) in Mz, TP, Bes, Pal.
(*e*) in Mz, TP, Pal, Mu.
(*f*) in TP, Pal, Mu.
(*g*) in Val.

but Fi omits CLII *c*, *d*; Mz omits CXLII *b*, CXLVIII *b*, CLII *d*, CLIV *c*, *d*; Pal omits CLI *b*, CLI *f*, *g*, *h*; CLII *d*, CLIII *d*; Mu (besides CXLVII and CXLVIII) omits CLI *h*, CLII *d*.

Val. has an unsystematic list of twenty-one items; among them only two are unusual, there is (rewritten) for a Doctor, Optaui et datus est (Sap. vii. 7–11) . . . . cum illa: and added at the end is Ad quem angelorum (Heb. i. 13–ii. 3) . . . . confirmata est.

---

[a] The later additions made in the body of the Corbie MS. (pp. 25, 66) present no novelties; two are references only to Epistles in the Sanctorale: five are in fact in the *Commune*; so is the sixth (St. James), but it is wrongly cited as being 'in antea'.

[b] CXLVII *a* is also added here.

Votives

TP is modern in plan, and methodical: it omits a few and adds the following:

Mr. Nemo militans (2 Tim. ii. 4–10) A 229.
Mrr. Metuentes d. (Ecclus. ii. 7–13) .... in veritate.
Respondens unus (Rev. vii. 13–17) A 127.
Conf. Scietis quia misi (Mal. ii. 4–7) A 226.
Omnis pontifex = CLVIII c.
Doctor. Rigabo hortum (Ecclus. xxiv. 42–xxv. 2) .... consentientes.

Bes has a very small Commune and that almost entirely made up of cues.

Qt, Ver, and Bob remain. These three Comes MSS. have practically the same[a] Commune which mainly agrees with the Standard, but omits CLI c, g, h, and CLIV c, d, and adds *Corde enim creditur* = CXXXVIII for an Apostle and *In omnibus requiem* = CXVIII for a Virgin.

§ 13. So far as Votives are concerned, the tendency of the Epistle-lists at first is more to shrink than to develop. The Standard had thirty-two entries, several fewer than on the corresponding occasions of the Earlier Series (We), as is shown above: but it made up the number again by adding fresh occasions. Others of the Epistle-lists have a very small collection: Fi has seven, Mz six, Val only one, Bes has seventeen, several of which are new. TP is developed to a stage which lies beyond the limits of our enquiry.[b]

The Comes MSS. follow the same line. Pal, Pam, Qf, Bob, have very few: Theo has a score, including some of the novelties. On the other hand, Aud, Mu, Qt, and Ver (alike as usual), have a fairly complete set taken from the Standard series, and some interesting additions as well.[c]

[a] Bob omits also CLII d: and in all cases it is not clear whether CXLVII a or b is intended.

[b] The details follow, except for TP which can be found in Tommasi, v. 410–22.

(1) Fi CLV, CLVII b; CLX, CLXXIV. For St. Matthew, Egrotavit Ezechias (Is. xxxviii) xxiii. Agenda CLXXV a, b. Then follow SS. Simon and Jude CXLVIII c, a. 'Dom. de Trinitate' Gaudete (2 Cor. xiii. 11–13) .... omnibus vobis.

(2) Mz CLIX a, b; CLXXV a, b.

(3) Val CLXX: 'Ad poscenda angelica suffragia' Dixit .... Scribe (Rev. xix. 9, 10) .... adora.

(4) Bes CLX, CLIX; CLVII b, a, CLXII. 'Propria sacerdotis' Condelector (Rom. vii. 22–4) .... huius: and CLXV b, A 224, CLXXIV, CLXXII a, CLXVI. 'Ad poscendam serenitatem' LVIII. 'Pro fidelibus defunctis' CLXXV a. Audiui vocem .... Scribe (Rev. xiv. 13) .... sequuntur illos CLXXV b.

[c] The details are as follows:

(4) Pal CLIX a, b, CLXXV a, and Audiuimus .... Scribe (above).

(5) Aud has CLV–VIII, CLXII, CLXIV and CLXV, CLXVIII and CLXVII, CLXX, CLXIX,

§ 14. A new feature, however, begins to appear among the Votives in the shape of a scheme providing a mass for each day of a week, with a special intention. This appears in four of the Epistle-lists Fi, Val, TP, Bes as well as two of the Comes MSS. Pal, Qf. The scheme varies to some extent in the different MSS. The following list shows those of Pal, with additions (marked with *a*) from elsewhere.

Pal. Dominica. 'De trinitate'.
    i. Gaudete perfecti estote (2 Cor. xiii. 11–13) . . . . vobis.
    i *a*. O altitudo (Rom. xi. 33–6) . . . . Ipsi gloria in s. saec.
Feria ii 'De sapientia'.
    ii. Dixit Salomon, D. patrum (Sap. ix. 1–5) . . . . ancillae tuae.
Feria iii. 'De spiritu sancto'.
    iii. Unicuique (1 Cor. xii. 7–11) . . . . prout uult.

besides 'Pro ordinantibus', 'Pro Episcopo', 'In unius defuncti', 'In Agenda plurimorum', CLXXV, 'In Scrutinio'—'primo'—'secundo'—'tertio', CLXVI.

(6) Mu has CLV, CLVI, CLVII *a*. Then, after a gap, CLXXI, CLXXII *a*, *b*, CLXXIII, 'Ad missa pro helymosinam' *Qui parce* = CXVII, and Hoc est ieiunium (Is. lviii. 6) part of XXIV.

'Pro salute uiuorum' *Orationem faciebant* = XXXII *c*.

'Pro infirmo' CLXXIV and *Egrotauit Ezechias* = XXIII, CLXXV *a*, *b* with Sicut portauimus (1 Cor. xv. 49–).

(7) Pam has CLIX *a*, *b*, and Stetit Salomon (3 Reg. viii. 22). Then CLV. Not CLVI, but instead, Sacrificium salutare (Ecclus. xxxv. 2). Then CLVII *b*, *a*.

Lastly CLXXV *a*, *b*, with *Sicut portauimus* (above), Facta est super me LXVI*h, and Audiui uocem . . . . Scribe (above, p. 63).

(8) Qf has a few Votives among later additions at the end.

(9) Bob has CLIX *a*, *b*, CLX, CLV, CLVI, CLVII *b*, CLVIII, CLXI *b*, CLXXII, CLXIV, CLXXIV: the end is wanting.

(10) Theo. *Noli timere terra* (Joel ii. 21–6) A 223, not CLXVIII: CLXVI, XXIII, CLVIII *b*, CLV–VII, CLX, CLXII, CLXIX, CLXIV *c* with *Facite justitiam* (Jer. xxii. 3, 4) AA 221 and *Si iniquitates* (Jer. xiv. 7–9) A 224.

'In natale sacerdotum' Scietis quia misi (Mal. ii. 4–7) A 226.

'Missa qua sacerdos pro se canet' Scimus quod lex spiritalis (Rom. vii. 14–25) AA 54.

Then CLXXIII, CLXXIV, CLXXII *a*, CLXXV *a*, *b*, with xxv.

(11) Qt has CLV–CLVIII *c*: CLXI–CLXII, CLXIV–CLXVII. [Commune], CLXXV *a*, *b*: Conuertit rex Salomon (p. 32) with CLIX *a*, *b*. Then CLX: CLXIX with

    Nihil enim intulimus (p. 57).
    Recogitate J.C. (p. 56).
    Ad quem angelorum (p. 62).
    Festinemus ingredi (p. 56).

Then CLXX to CLXXIV with Audi fili verba mandati (cp. LXVI * *g* and LXXXVI *f*).

    'De conciliatione fratrum' Induite vos (p. 52).
    'Pro eleemosina' (*blank*)
    'Pro tribulatione' CLXIV *b*.

(12) Ver has the same: but after CLXXIV it is not legible.

Sanctorale

iii *a*. Benignus (Sap. i. 6, 7) .... habet vocis.
Feria iv. 'De angelis'.
iv. Dixit mihi Angelus (Rev. xix. 9, 10) .... adora.
Feria v. 'De caritate'.
v. Caritas patiens (1 Cor. xiii. 4–8) .... excidit.
Feria vi. 'De sancta cruce'.
vi. Mihi autem absit (Gal. vi. 14) .... mundo.
vi *a*. Christus factus est (Phil. ii. 8–11) .... dei patris.
Feria vii. 'De S. Maria'.
vii. Fortitudo et decor (Prov. xxxi. 25–9) .... uniuersas.
vii *a*. Ab initio et ante (Ecclus. xxiv. 14–16) .... detentio mea.

The corresponding Gospels in Pal are, Sun. **134**, Mon. Confiteor (Mt. xi. 25–30). Tues. **136**, Wed. **66** (Jo. v. 1–4). Thurs. Filioli (Jo. xiii. 33–5), Fri. Nemo (Jo. iii. 13–15), Sat. Extollens (Lu. xi. 27, 28): but in Qf Intrauit J. (Lu. x. 38).

Pal has i–vii. TP has i *a*, ii–v, vi *a*, vii. Fi ends with i only: the rest presumably is lost.

Val has for—
    Feria ii. 'De caritate' Gratia dei (2 Cor. xiii. 13) .... Amen.
    Feria iii. 'De caritate' = v.
    Feria iv. 'De spiritu Sancto' Notum nobis (1 Cor. xii. 3–11) .... prout uult.
    Feria v. 'De sapientia' i *a*.
    Feria vi. 'De cruce' vi *a*.
    Feria vii. 'De S. Maria' (erased).

Bes has i, ii, v, iii *a*, vi *a*, vii *a*, iv.
Qf had i (on a misplaced leaf), iv and vii *a*.
MS. has quite a different set (see p. 73).

§ 15. The comparison of the Sanctoralia of the various available MSS. presents greater difficulties. First it must be noted that the Epistle-books proper must, at this point, be considered separately from the Comes-lists, because the latter, in combining Epistle and Gospel together, have been much influenced by the highly developed Sanctorale of the Gospel-series. The separate treatment of the Comes is therefore reserved for Chapter VI.

(*a*) In the Epistle-lists the small Sanctorale of the Standard-series remained dominant; and it kept the Saints-days few, until the insistence of later developments broke down its exclusiveness. Meanwhile, it had provided twenty-two entries for Saints: the three that follow Christmas, Sebastian, Agnes and Agatha, Philip and James, *Invention of Holy Cross*, John Baptist with Vigil, Peter with Vigil, Paul alone with

66 *Development*

Vigil, *Octave of the Apostles*, Felicitas (Aug. 1), Lawrence and Vigil, *Assumption, Passion of John Baptist*, Michaelmas, Andrew and Vigil.

All of these, except those italicized, appear in the earlier list (We) together with Silvester, John and Paul, Sixtus, and, as an afterthought, Sabina.

(*b*) The Corbie MS., whence comes the Standard-series, has the following additions in the body of the list: James, Bartholomew, Nativity of the B.V.M., Exaltation of Holy Cross, Matthew, and Vigil, Simon and Jude, and Vigil—eight in all besides those added in one or other Appendix.

(*c*) Fi adds Silvester, Purification, Vitalis, Processus and Martinian, James, and Vigil of the Assumption, the Nativity of the B.V.M., Cornelius and Cyprian, Matthew, and Vigil, All Saints, and Vigil, Thomas—thirteen in all: and it omits the Vigil of Paul, as do most other lists.[a]

(*d*) Mz adds all those in Fi, except Vitalis, Processus and Martinian, James, Cornelius and Cyprian, and Thomas. It adds also Simon and Jude, with Vigil, as Corbie.

(*e*) C is a fragment covering mainly some parts of the year when few Saints are to be expected, especially Lent and Easter week. There is a gap where LXXVIII SS. Philip and James and LXXX the Invention of the Cross might be expected; but after Pentecost the Sundays called Pent$^{5-11}$ are found in place following one another without any feast of St. John Baptist, CI, CII, or SS. Peter and Paul CIV–CVII, CIX intervening. It seems therefore possible that in this Epistle-book the Saints already were gathered apart into a Sanctorale.

§ 16. A certain number of new lessons are brought into use by these additional entries; and it will be well to have a combined list of the new passages as well as the new days in these three MSS.

S. Silvester. *Ecce sacerdos* (CL *a*). Fi, Mz.
Purification. Ecce ego mittam (Mal. iii. 1–4) A 25.
Processus and Martinian. *Stabunt iusti* = LXXVIII. Fi.
James.   *Justum deduxit* (CLI *d*) Corb.
  Benedictio domini = CXXXVII. Fi.
Bartholomew. *Jam non estis* (CXLVIII *a*) Corb.
Vigil of the Assumption. Dominus possedit me (Prov. viii. 22–35) .... salutem a domino, Fi, Mz.
Nativ. B.V.M. *In omnibus requiem* = CXVIII. Corb.
  Ego quasi vitis (Ecclus. xxiv. 23–31) A 179.
  Sapientia laudabit (CLIV *c*) Mz.

[a] It has survived only in We, the Standard, and the Comes MSS. Aud, Mu, Qt, Ver.

Sanctorale

Exaltation of H. Cross. *Hoc sentite* = LXI. Corb, and as Cornelius and Cyprian in Fi.
Vigil of Matthew. *Beatus vir qui inuenit* (CXLVII a) Corb, Fi, Mz.
Day. *Unicuique nostrum* (CXLVIII b). Corb, Fi, Mz.
Vigil of Simon and Jude. *Justorum animae* (CLIII a) Corb, Mz.
Day. *Scimus enim quoniam* (CXLVIII c) Corb, Mz.[a]
Vigil of All Saints. Et ecce ego J. vidi in medio (Rev. v. 6–12). A 189. Fi, Mz.
Day. Et ecce ego J. Vidi alterum (Rev. vii. 2–12) A 190. Fi, Mz.
Thomas. *Beatus vir qui inuentus* (CXLVII b)

There are also a few changes to be noted as regards original days. Mz omits Agnes and Agatha, and the Invention of H. Cross. It alters Vig Asc to CXLVIII b, and the Passion of St. John Baptist has, in both Fi and Mz, not CXX, but *Sancti ludibria* A 161.

Note that the other three Epistle-lists, being of later date, exhibit greatly developed Sanctoralia. Two of them, TP and Bes, have the Sanctorale separate from the Temporale—that is to say, they have broken away in this respect from the arrangement of the Old Roman Capitulary. It was thought worth while to bring them into this inquiry, partly because of the evidence that they could contribute about the ancient parts of the list, and partly because they show the development of the provision for Fridays (pp. 58–60). But it is not germane to our purpose to describe their Sanctoralia in detail.

Val, however, has not broken away, but has kept to the old arrangement in regard to the Saints-days. Besides, as an Italian MS. of the 10th century it deserves further attention. See the account given of the MS. below (p. 68). Here it is enough to note that to most of the additional Saints are given Epistles already included in the Standard-series.

THE MANUSCRIPTS

(a) Lectionaries

We. Würzburg. See p. 1: and more fully vol. II, p. 74.

Corbie. From which the Standard list is taken. See the account of the MS. above at p. 25.

Alc. Paris, Bibl. Ntle. MS. Latin 9452. See the description above Chapter III. A MS. of the 9th century from Chartres.

[a] Fi has in an Appendix CXLVIII c and a for Vigil and Day.

68   *Development*

Fi. Cambridge, Fitzwilliam Museum Library, MS. Maclean 30. An Epistle-lectionary of the 10th century, and German in origin with a Byzantine ivory in the binding. ff. 152+2. 266×197.
 f. i^v. The letter of Jerome to Constantius. See p. 74.
 f. 2. 'In Christi nomine incipiunt lectiones per circulum anni.'
 Note, before LXX add Theoph[5] with Induite vos (p. 52). After Pasch[1] add Vitalis with CLI *b*. At CXIV the Machabees as well as Felicitas. XL[3]v and XL[4]v are interchanged. At Decoll. reference is made to the Commune for *Sancti ludibria* Alc 161 which is not there. Oct Pent is given CXIII as well as XCIV.
 f. 139. Commune sanctorum, and Votives, with additions and one also for St. Matthew with XXIII.
 SS. Simon and Jude with CXLVIII*c* and *a*.
 Trinity Sunday, Gaudete, perfecti estote (2 Cor. xiii. 11–13) . . . . omnibus vobis.[a]

Mz. Mainz, Domschatz, Epistle-lectionary of the 10th century; probably of Mainz.
 f. 1^v. 'Incipit liber comitum'.
 After Advent there is a 'Vigilia omnium Apostolorum' CXLVII*a*, with the Natale following, having CXLVIII*a*, VI*a*, CXLVIII *c* and CXLIX, and the rest of a Commune Sanctorum (see § 12); but no Votives except Dedication, CLIX*a*, *b* and 'Agenda mortuorum', CLXXV*a*, *b*.

Val. Rome, Vallicellana MS. c. 10, contains a Gospel-series of the 12th century.
 ff. 1–127; with later additions (f. 128) and three blank folios.
 ff. 132–8. A leaf of an Early Psalter followed by the Mass-Canon & some masses of the Dead.
 ff. 139–280. Epistle-Book of the 10th century.
 A–F^8 G^{14} H–Q^8 R^6 a^7 Aa^{8+2} Bb–Rr^8 Ss^4.
 The book hails from the Monastery of Valcassoriana near Norcia in Umbria, as is shown by the entry (May 23) 'In nl. S. Euthicii abb.' with two Epistles from the Common. Other notable entries are St. Martina (Jan. 1); St. Michael on Monte Gargano May 8; the Transfiguration with a Vigil.
 The Rogation days have special Epistles.
 The list begins with Advent; and at the end of the Proper, after St. Andrew comes Trinity Sunday with O altitudo (Rom. xi. 33–6) . . . . ipsi gloria in s. saec.
 Then follows the Commune, to which are appended Epistles for LXX iv and LX iv (p. 56) two Votives (p. 63) and Epistles for week-days (p. 65).

---

[a] There is said to be at Leipzig a similar MS. of the 10th century, viz. *Stadtbibliothek*, MS. cxc, but it is not clear how far the similarity goes.

The MSS.

The following is a summary of the Sanctorale.

Silvester. CXLVII *b* and CL *a*.
Martina. XVIII.
Felix. CLI *a*.
Prisca. CLIV *b*.
Sebastian. XVII.
Fabian. CLI *b*.
Agnes. CLIV *a*.
Vincent. CXXXVII.
Purification. A 25.
Agatha. XVIII.
Valentine. CLI *d*.
Gregory. CLVIII *b, c*.
Benedict. CLI *b*.
Annunciation. CXLIII *a*.
George. CLI *e*.
Litania Maior. LXXXII.
Vitalis. A 229.
Philip and James. LXXVIII.
Alexander, Ev. and Th. XCIV.
In Sancti Angeli (May 8). A 182 (Monte Gargano).
Nereus and A. CLI *c*.
In tribus litaniis = XCIX, CIII. A 221.
Eutychius abb. (May 23). CXLIX and CXLVII *b*.
Marcellinus and P. CLII *b*.
Basilides, C. and N. CLIII *a*.
Mark and M. CLIII *b*.
John Baptist. CI, CII.
John and Paul. A. 127.
Peter. CIV, CV.
Paul. CVII.
Processus and M. CIX.
Oct. Apostolorum. CXLVIII *b*.
Septem Fratres. CLIII *d*.

Simon and Jude[a]
Vinc: Petri. CV.
Machabees. CXIV.
Vig Transfig. Ego Johannes vidi septem candelabra (Rev. i. 13–18) ... viuens in s. saec.
Transfig. Dabo autem operam. (2 Pet. i. 15–19) ... cordibus n. and CLIV *c*.
Cyriac. CLIII *a*.
Lawrence. CXVI, CXVII.
Eusebius. Ne quis vos decipiat. A 239.
Vig Assumpt. Osculetur me (Cant. i. 1 &c.) .... decora.
Assumption. CXVIII.
Decollatio (rewritten). Ego Johannes vidi ang. (Rev. xx. 1–?) .... cum illo in s. saec.
Nat. B. Mary. A 179.
Cornelius and C. CLII *b*.
Exalt. Cross. Mysterium quod (Col. i. 26–9) .... virtute.
Matthew. CLIV *d* and CXLVIII *a*.
Cosmas and D. CLIII *a*.
Michael. CXXX.
Jerome. CXLVII *a*.
Mark. CL *c*.
Simon and Jude. CXLVIII *a*.
All Saints. A 189, 190.
Four Crowned. XCIV.
Martin. CL *a*.
Cecilia. CLIV *b*.
Clement. CL *b*.
Saturninus. A 229.
Andrew. CXXXVII, CXXXVIII.

TP. Rome, Vatican Library, MS. Palatine 497. An Epistle-lectionary late in both style and date; probably of the 12th century, German in origin, perhaps from Trier.
The Sanctorale is separate; and there is a Commune.
This MS. was utilized by Tommasi: it is called P in his combined lectionary (*Opera*, vol. v, 320–   ); but only excerpts are included.

Bes. Rome, Vatican Library, MS. Borgia 359. Epistle-lectionary and Gradual of the late 11th century from the Canons of St. Stephen's, Besançon.

---

[a] Both date and lesson are unusual. Simon Petrus seruus et apostolus J. C. et judas zelotes his qui aequalem (2 Pet. i. 1–   ). All is rewritten and incomplete: the next page is almost completely torn out.

f. 3ᵛ. List of Bishops.
ff. 4–132. Epistle-Book with (f. 111) a separate Sanctorale and Commune.
f. 135. 'Christus vincit'.
f. 136– . Gradual.

At f. 41 is given the *Ordo* for the Procession on Palm Sunday, with notation.
After f. 22, there is a gap extending from the end of June to October 30.
Note at Feb. 22. In Antiochia Cath. S. Petri, Petrus apostolus (1 Pet. i. 1–7) . . . . reuelatione d. n. J. C.
Feb. 24. Matthias, Exurgens Petrus . . . . (Acts i. 15–26) . . . . undecim Ap.
June 16. Ferreol and Ferrutius CIX.
June 17. Antidius CLI *b*.
June 28. Irenaeus CLIII *b*.
Oct. 25. Quintin A 229.
Nov. 1 or 3. Benignus. Benedicentes d. exaltate (Ecclus. xliii. 33 and l. 31) . . . vestigium eius est.

C. Cambridge, a MS. in the private possession of Sir Sydney Cockerell, who was kind enough to tell me about it and show it me, just as this book was taking final shape. It is very incomplete containing mainly the Lenten part from XL³ii to Easter, some parts between Easter-week and Ascension, and two smaller fragments containing most of the contents from Pent⁴ to Pent¹⁴, which are peculiar, and most of the September Embertide. But C. is of special interest for several reasons. It comes from a church of St. Cecilia, probably that of Rome, for many small features show special knowledge of Rome. After Easter-even is added on a blank space in a more or less contemporary hand (? of the 11th century) a malediction on any thief 'quicunque istum librum epistolarum ab ecclesia S. virginis Cecilie rapuerit', &c. Most notable is the amount and elaboration of the music at the closing lessons of Easter-even LXVI*. Also there instead of (*g*) there is the lesson *Surgite et ascendamus* (Jer. xxxi. 6–14) as in Ver. The Station of Pasch¹ is ad S. Pancratium, as in some later books.[a] The Litania maior is placed between Pasch³ and Pasch⁴, together with the Roman observance of St. Mark's day 'eodem die S. Marci' with the cue of CXLVII *b*.

After Pasch⁵ follow the Gallican Rogation-days thus: 'In tribus letaniis', Feria ii. Collecta ad S. Mariam maiorem, Statio ad S. Johannem with *Humiliamini* XLIX, Feria iii. Collecta ad S. Savinam, Statio ad S. Paulum *Omnes unianimes* CIII. Vig Ascensionis d. *Unicuique nostrum* CXLVIII *b*. The places prescribed for the Monday and Tuesday correspond with those in Tommasi's edition of the Gradual;[b] but for the Wednesday here there is no mention of places.

Other peculiarities of this MS. have been already noted elsewhere.

[a] Including Ordo Romanus XI (*c*. 1140). See vol. I, pp. 20, 23.
[b] *Opera*, v, pp. 110, 111.

The MSS.

(b) Comes MSS. (i)

Pal. Rome, Vatican MS. Palatine 510. A Comes of a fairly early type but not primitive. It has a Commune; and in the Gospels it draws upon the 'Alternative Series'. ff. 247, 220 × 160.

The Comes for the year is followed by provision for a liturgical week, a Commune, and Votives for Dedication and Agenda Mortuorum.

Then come additions: for the Vigil of St. Lawrence with Epistle cxvi and Gospels 191, 186. For the Nativity of the B.V.M., with *Dominus possedit me* (p. 66), and the Genealogy.

The Canticle 'Benedictus' with neums.

Aud. Chartres MS. 24. A fine MS. of the Comes, probably written in the 9th century at Tours, and used at St. Père.

p. 1. Incipit prologus libri comitis S. Hieronymi presbyteri missum ad Constantium constantinopolitanum episcopum.

Quanquam licenter....

Inserted in the interstices of the pattern on p. 1 are letters making up the name AUDRADUS. One of this name was among the community, at St. Martin of Tours, *c.* 820, and later Chorepiscopus of Sens.

p. 4. 'Incipiunt lectiones libri comitis anni circuli.'

There are neums added to vi. A system of numbering is attached to the entries, but only parts of it are preserved. Naturally it differs from the standard numbering. Divergence seems to begin with No. 7 and goes on increasingly, mainly through the addition of Saints-days and Ferias, but also by omissions. It differs also from the numbering in Alc.

After the end of the year come the Votives beginning with No. 230 = CLV. After the 'Agenda mortuorum' are the three scrutinies. They are followed by 'Pro sterilitate pluviae'. An Appendix follows for 17 more Saints, all of them familiar, and several lessons for a Virgin. The list then ends with the Genealogy for the Vigil of Epiphany.

See a further description of the MS. and scribe by Dom. A. Wilmart (with a facsimile of p. 1) in *Comptes rendus de l'académie des inscr.* of Paris, for Nov. 13, 1925, pp. 290–8. Also *Jahrbuch*, vi. 341.

Qt. Paris, Bibl. Ntle. MS. Latin 9451. A 'codex purpureus' of the Comes, finely written, but carelessly edited: in double columns and not very legible. ff. 199. 312 × 220.

ff. 1, 2 blank.

f. 3. In nomine.... incipit prologus libri comitum b. Hieronymi presb. ad Constantium Constantinopolitanum Episcopum: lege feliciter. Quanquam licenter &c.....

f. 4. The lectionary.

There are slight traces of a numbering of the items at the beginning.

The Votives follow on at the end of the year, and the Commune comes in the middle of them, followed by the Four *initia* of the Gospels to be read at the 'Effeta' of Baptism. These are also in Tommasi, *Opera*, v. 451.

Then an appendix makes provision for other Saints-days and Holy-days: among them are 'Pascha Annotina' with Dignus es (Apoc. iv. 11); Litania maior, Domine exercituum (Is. xxxvii. 16); SS. Sixtus Hippolytus and Cassian cix; the martyrs Adrian Protus and Hyacinth. *Nihil intulimus* (p. 57); St. Martin, Omnis scriptura (2 Tim. iii. 16, 17).

Two Michaelmas additions are included, one for the day (Alc 182) and one for the octave, Nonne omnes sunt administratorii (Heb. i. 14–ii. 4).

Ver. Verona, Chapter Library MS. LXXXII. A Comes very similar in many ways to Qt: but the first two quires are lacking.

Collation: thirty-seven quires usually of eight, but the first two are gone. One has ten; one has only seven; and the last has only four. A leaf is lost after f. 260 in the Votives.

The MS. shows large parts of a system of numbering its items, not like others.

The Sunday 'Oct Pent' is called 'In nl. Sanctorum'. Cp. p. 30.

After Adv⁴ is 'In vigilia nl. domini ad nonam *hic demitte revertere ad initium libri*:' thus noting the change of custom which had transferred the Vigil Mass to the end of the series.

(b) Comes MSS. (ii)

Mu. Besançon MS. 184. A Comes-list occupies ff. 57–73, dating from the end of the 8th or beginning of the 9th century.

It has been printed with full commentary by Dom Wilmart in *Revue Bénédictine*, xxx (1913), 25–69. It originated probably from Murbach.

Qf. Paris, Bibl. Ntle. MS. Nouv. Acq. Latin 1541. A Comes from Trier, late in style, fine in execution, written in gold and silver on purple, with illumination.

f. 1ᵛ In nomine domini incipiunt epistole cum evangeliis ordinatim recitande in diebus privatis seu in sanctorum nataliciis.

DOM. I IN ADVENTU DOMINI.

f. 3 a leaf is inserted concerning the relics of St. Maximin of Trier.

At Pent. iii. *Si infra Pentecosten euenerit ieiunium* iv^{ti} *mensis legantur hę duę lectiones. Sin autem una earum. Et iv feria, et vi, ac Sabbato cantetur* Alleluia, *nec flectantur genua.* Then follow cx. Alia cix.

f. 174ᵛ. Incipiunt Epistolae cum euangeliis ordinatim recitande in sanctorum nataliciis (Silvester-Andrew), followed by Dedication and a few other Votives, but no Commune.

Pam. The Comes printed by J. Pamelius in his *Liturgicon Ecclesiae Latinae*, vol. ii, pp. 1–61 (Köln, 1571). He used a lectionary of his own church, the Cathedral of Bruges, and some MSS. of the Chapter at Köln, brought to his notice by M. Hittorp.

The 'Comes'

Bob. Milan, Ambrosian Library MS. C. 228 inf. A Comes presumably from Bobbio, or its neighbourhood, as it has St. Columban at Nov. 23. The Sanctorale is closely allied to the Hadrianum. ff. 183.
At the end of the year there follow a Commune and a set of Votives which is incomplete, ending in No. CLXXIV.
ff. 182, 183 are added leaves, intended to supply the Johannine set of Gospels for the Thursdays in Lent. In other respects also the list has been altered itself in conformity with later usage.
The Gospel of St. John Evang. is noted in neums.

Theo. For this MS. see Chapter VIII.

MS. Munich, MS. Clm. 14452. A book of Epistles and Gospels of the 11th or even 12th century, in date, but earlier in contents, and with some notation. It has divided the Saints-days into blocks, but added very little to the Standard list. The Sanctorale of the summer should follow the Temporale: then comes f. 189 Commune and f. 209 Votives, including a week of private masses.[a] But ff. 218–44 are wrongly bound at the end: they should precede the Commune.
ff. 244. 238 × 180.

Bml. Oxford, Bodleian Library MS. 19413. A book of Epistles and Gospels (*B.M.L.* 238) of W. German origin dating from the late 11th or early 12th century. There is a developed Sanctorale, but it is made up of references. The Commune follows. ff. 195. 218 × 155.

TQ. Rome, Vatican Library MS. Palat. 44. Called Q by Tommasi (*Opera*, v. 430–). It is a New Test. with tables of Gospels and Epistles. It is negligible as regards Epistles, for there are none after Epiph^s. For the Gospels see Tommasi.

CHAPTER V

The 'Comes'

WE can now take up the puzzling question of the Comes, its origin and its nature, which has been postponed hitherto; and this inquiry will facilitate the consideration of the Sanctorale of the Epistle-lists, which was left over from p. 65.

The term 'Comes' is found in Carolingian days, and it is applied to a collection of lessons for mass. At a much earlier date, in an inventory of church goods of 471,[b] it is found in close con-

---

[a] Thus: Pro seipso.
In annivers. presb.
De quacunque tribulatione.
Pro peccatis.
Pro amico viuente.
Pro infirmis.

[b] The 'Charta Cornutiana' *L.P.* (ed. Duchesne), i, p. cxlvi.

nexion with Gospel-book, Apostle, and Psalter. But it is not easy to interpret this piece of evidence. The name Comes appears, indeed, together with church-books; but since Gospel-book and Epistle-book are mentioned independently, the term 'Comes', as used there, may be thought to refer to something quite different. In the 9th century the name is fairly common, but it seems to have gone out again from the usage of the Roman rite, though it survived in Spain.[a]

While, however, the term disappeared from the MSS. and their headings, it survived in literary references to the subject made by the liturgists. Berno of Reichenau (†1014) says that St. Jerome arranged the Lectionary 'ut ipsius testatur prologus appositus in capite eiusdem "comitis"—sic eum appellavit'.[b] Bernold of Konstanz at the end of the 11th century has an echo of this statement;[c] and, more explicitly, Ralph of Tongres ascribes to St. Jerome the existing series of mass-lessons, 'ut in libro qui Comes dicitur habetur: ut ipse ait scribens ad Constantium episcopum.'[d]

The single source of all this tradition is the Letter of St. Jerome to Constantius. The MSS. themselves in a certain number of cases prefix this letter to the lessons in the lectionary.

So along both lines of evidence we come to examine that document.

Six texts of it have been available for that purpose.[e] The variations are of little importance except for the heading. It runs in the best-known form thus:[f]

(*a*) In nomine S. et individuae trinitatis
(*b*) incipit epistola S. Hieronymi missa ad Constantium.
(*c*) Praefatio libri sequentis qui Comes appellatur.

This is the form in which it has been most widely current: but (*a*) is often wanting, or else shorter: (*c*) seems peculiar to this form: while (*b*) is better attested in this shape:[g]

---

[a] See the *Liber Comicus* of Toledo in *Anal. Maredsolana* (ed. Morin, 1893).

[b] *Libellus*, c. 1, in *P.L.* cxlii. 1057.

[c] *Micrologus*, c. xxv, *P.L.* cli. 999.

[d] *De canonum observ.*, c. xxiii. Cp. a mention in Sigebert's Chronicle for the year 688; in *P.L.* clx. 130.

[e] The MSS. are Corbie, Fi, Qt, Aud, Mu, and there is besides the text printed by D'Achery, from a copy sent to him by Chifflet: *Spicilegium*, vol. iii. 301: *P.L.* xxx. 486: reprinted by Tommasi, *Opera* (ed. Vezzosi), v. 319. Dom Morin has dealt with the matter in *R.B.* vii. 416, xv. 241, and xxx. 25, 124. He quotes also from two Vatican MSS.—Ottoboni 478 and Latin 317—which are later transcripts from older MSS. [f] D'Achery's text.

[g] Corbie, Qt and Aud.

The 'Comes' 75

'Incipit prologus libri comitis[a] S. Hieronymi presbyteri missus ad Constantium.'[b]

The text of the letter is printed here from the Corbie MS. as given by Staerk with the heading last mentioned. The document in Fi has almost exactly the same text. The variants are small except in the closing words. The form in Theotinchus is an adaptation made for that MS.[c]

INCIPIT PROLOGUS LIBRI COMITIS SANCTI HIERONIMI PRESBITERI
MISSUS AD CONSTANTIUM

Quanquam licenter adsumatur in opere congregatio caelestium lectionum, et ipsum opusculum ab ecclesiasticis viris Comes quidem [soleat] appellari: quod duobus modis fieri arbitror, aut pro consuetudine unius cuiusque ecclesie, secundum quod et varium hoc ipsum descriptionis genus esse dignoscitur, aut certe pro uoluntate studiosi lectoris qui, si fieri possit, quicquid in Scripturis divinis mirabiliter fulget, quidquid in praeceptis moralibus copiosum est totum paruo in corpore adunatum habere desiderant, paupertatis necessitate: Ego tamen, iuuante Christo, ingenio ut potui, et maxime occasione oblata, quia id a me fieri uoluisti, Constanti venerabilis mihi frater, ita hoc opus, etsi minus instructus, adsumpsi, ut tanta exce[r]ptorum permixtio intelligentiae caput causamque rationabilem habere uideatur.

Nam cum *omnis scriptura diuinitus inspirata,* ut ait apostolus, *utilis sit ad docendum, ad erudiendum ad iustitiam, ut perfectus sit homo dei, ad omne opus bonum instructus*; et *quaecumque sunt [h]actenus scripta, ad nostram doctrinam scripta sunt, ut per patientiam et consolationem scripturarum spem habeamus,* quid breuius, quid utilius censui[d] quam ut, ex tanta diuinorum [librorum copia], singulis[d] festiuitatibus quod aptum ex his vel competens esset, excerperem, et quodam modo distinctissime collocarem.

Incipiens itaque a natiuitate Christi, quod est VIII Kal. Januarias in uigiliis ad Nonam, per ordinem quem assidue in ecclesia didiceram lectiones utriusque Testamenti simplicibus ministraui.

Porro editione illa quam ex hebraicis uoluminibus in latinum translatam esse constat in hunc quippe modum que uel cuiusque prophete lectio presenti festiuitati congruat, quid Apostoli doceant, uel ad eundem titulum quid Euangelii adnuntiet auctoritas,

---

[a] 'libri comitis' is omitted in Fi Mu. Qt reads 'comitum'.

[b] Qt Fi Ottob. add 'Constantinopolitanum episcopum'. Aud has, and Vatic. Latin 317 has (over erasure), 'Constantiae episcopum': Qt adds 'lege feliciter'.

[c] In Christi nomine anni circuli liber comitis incipit, auctus, &c. See below, ch. VIII.   [d-d] quam extenta singulis divinorum.

dudum, vertente iam anno, per omnes dies festos ecclesie opportune censui omnia secundum tempus esse legenda.

Sed et nonnulla alia aedificationis causa multa illic adgregata sunt, atque suis appellationibus inserta; Idest in capite Quadragesime de abstinentia sanctorum et sobrietate. Item in Quadragesima de penitentia, de pudicitia, de remissione inimicitiarum vel alia multa. Haec enim omnia ad multorum equidem utilitatem, petitionibus tuis oboediens scribere curaui, uenerabilis mihi et amantissime frater.   Explicit prologus.

This letter to Constantius is a puzzle. The Latin is bad, and the style obscure. It was largely copied by Alan of Farfa (†770) in his preface to his Homiliary[a] (as Dom Morin has found it in a MS. at Munich), but without any acknowledgement. So we do not know what Alan thought about either the sender or the recipient of the letter.

No convincing theory on this point has yet been put out,[b] but it is fairly safe to assume that the letter is a pseudonymous production of the early part of the 8th century. It was a time when great names were being attached to different parts of the liturgical tradition, in order to add weight and credit to them as they spread into the new areas. It is, of course, possible that St. Jerome may have made for Pope Damasus some systematic list of Epistles and Gospels: but it cannot have been any such list as that which we find with this letter to Constantius prefixed. The nature of the contents both in Temporale and Sanctorale would prove this—to say nothing of the wide divergence that exists in plan between early Epistle-list and early Gospel-list.

We fall back on the text of the letter itself for information, and note thus:

1. The name 'Comes' is taken as meaning a collection of scriptural passages; it may be made either to correspond with what is read in church, or else to serve as a biblical compendium for a poor student.
2. The compiler is presenting his 'comes' to the venerable and dearly beloved brother who had urged him to make it.
3. So he has gone through the Bible and the yearly course, excerpting passages from Prophet, Apostle, and Gospel suitable for particular feasts, and has arranged them for orderly reading.
4. His series begins with Christmas Eve at 'hora nona'.

[a] *R.B.* vii. 417. Only the Incipit is in *P.L.* lxxxix. 1197.
[b] *R.B.* xv. 241 gives an attempt of Dom Morin to find a suitable identification.

5. It includes a prophetic lesson, where suitable to the feast, an Epistle, and a Gospel for the course of the year.
6. Also the compiler has included in Lent, for edification's sake, a number of passages on moral questions.

This letter being prefixed to a number of lectionaries, the question arises how far it belongs to them, or how far they owe their origin to the work described by the writer.

We find it prefixed—
 (i) to a MS. which bears otherwise the name of Comes, and contains both Epistles and Gospels (Aud);
 (ii) to another which does not use the word 'Comes' otherwise than in the Letter, e.g. Qt;
 (iii) to lectionaries which contain the Epistles only, giving them in full, e.g. Corbie and Fi;
 (iv) to a Capitulary which is a list only, and does not contain any lessons in full, e.g. Mu.

Here is considerable diversity: and similar diversity prevails about the use of the term Comes in MSS. which do not contain the Letter at all.

Mz has the Epistles in full, headed 'Incipit liber comitum'.

Alc has the same; avoids the term in the main heading; but it is used, in the Preface to the Appendix, as the term descriptive of the main Lectionary (p. 45).

Theo has both Epistles and Gospels headed 'In Christi nomine anni circulo liber comitis incipit, &c.'

The *Collectiones in Epistolas et Evangelia*[a] of Smaragdus (early 9th century) is called in the Preface 'hic comitis liber'. The contents correspond fairly closely with the Standard series of Epistles, so far as they go: but they do not go much beyond the Sundays of the year, a few of the week-days in Lent, a dozen Saints-days, and a tiny Commune.

The Comes in fullest form seems then to have comprised:
1. The letter of Jerome.
2. An index of the days concerned.
3. The lectionary containing in full, or only by reference,
 (*a*) lessons from O.T.
 (*b*) lessons from N.T., other than the Gospels.
 (*c*) Gospel-lessons.

From this diversity it is evident that the term 'Comes' is not very precise.[b] Indeed, no MS. has, so far, emerged which corresponds

---
[a] *P.L.* cii. 15.
[b] It seems to have been applied to another kind of Service-book, perhaps a Missal, or Gradual; for a leaf has been found among bindings at Monte Cassino on which

closely with the description given in the Letter. The letter, therefore, ill-fits the MSS. with which it is associated. The term best fits those which have both Epistles and Gospels in full. It is, however, applied readily to Epistle-books; but not, apparently, to any Book of Gospels only.

The capitularies existed independently and previously to any use of the term Comes, just as they survived when it became extinct. The existence of a 'Comes' is then merely an episode in the history. Probably the course of the episode may be reconstructed somewhat as follows. At some stage in the development of the two lectionaries, prescribing the Epistles and the Gospels, some one produced the book as described in the Letter and issued it, with the title 'Comes' (Companion), and with the pseudonymous epistle of St. Jerome as *envoi*. It was a bold send-off, and for the time successful. A volume containing all the mass-lessons was found handy, and became popular. Where the church already had its Gospel-book, it was still convenient at any rate to have a separate collection of the Epistles such as were included in the Comes: and so the Lectionary, containing Epistles alone, acquired also the name of Comes.

The episode, apparently, was a short one. This term 'Comes' flourished in the 9th century, but it does not seem to have been so applied earlier,[a] nor to have survived much later,[b] except in the tradition of the Commentators, who could not fail to repeat like parrots the reference to St. Jerome. It does not regularly figure in the lists of usual church-books given in the Carolingian Capitularies. There is, however, one instance to be found. In one schedule of the things which clergy must learn, the eleventh item is, 'evangelium intelligere seu lectiones libri comitis'.[c]

Advent begins thus: 'In Christi nomine incipit liber comite composito a b. papa Gregorio et papa Damasus, et Hieronymo presbitero. In primis de Adventum domini. Introitus.' See *Bibl. Cassinensis* (1873), i. 180.

[a] The signs of early date, like the omission of the Lenten Thursdays, are wanting, and the transference of the Vigil Mass of Christmas from the end to the beginning of the list has already taken place.

[b] Lectionarius is also the usual word in the early catalogues published by G. Becker, *Catalogi Bibliothecarum Antiqui* (Bonn, 1885). The combined books of Epistles and Gospels appear in the St. Riquier list (of 831°) as 'lectionarii epistolarum et evangeliorum mixtim et ordinate compositi' (p. 28) or 'lectionarius plenarius a supradicto Albino ordinatus'. (Cp. p. 29, No. 27.) Note also at p. 36 'Librum comiti' at Köln; p. 37 at Clingen 'Librum comitis'; p. 51 St. Gall has 'Expositum super lectiones comitis pleniter per totum anni circulum legendum'. But the later lists have no such entries. The name seems to have gone out, even though the book continued into the 12th century.

[c] *Capitularia*, ed. Boretius (*M.G.H.*), vol. i, p. 235.

The 'Comes'

This account of the vogue of the term does not, therefore, add probability to the view that Jerome wrote the letter ascribed to him. The term, moreover, is not strictly in place when it is given to the Epistle-book of Alcuin by his editor. Whether Alcuin himself also used the term for a mere Epistle-book cannot be decided.

CHAPTER VI
The Sanctorale of the Comes

WE can now resume (from p. 65) the consideration of the Sanctorale of the Epistles, as it is exhibited in the Comes MSS. It has been greatly affected by being mated with the Gospel-list, for the small list of Saints included in the Epistle-book did not fit well with the greatly larger list in the Gospel-book. Two different policies seem to have been followed whenever it was that the project of combining (or at least reconciling) the two lists began. For one group of Comes (Pal, Aud, Qt, Ver) gives the major influence to the Epistle-list, and tries to assimilate the Gospel-list downwards to it. The other group (Mu, Qf, Pam, Bob) takes the opposite line, filling out the Epistle-list to assimilate it to the Gospel-list.

§ 1. The first group adds very little to the Epistles, being content for a good many occasions to provide no Epistle at all, but only a Gospel. The second group makes larger additions to the contents of the list, and provides an Epistle as well as the Gospel for each occasion, even if it be only by drawing on the Commune.

The procedure differs, however, in the four MSS. of the first group as regards some detailed points, thus:

(*a*) Pal. When Pal is compared with the Standard, it is observed that the Purification, Vig. of Assumption, Cornelius and Cyprian, Matthew with Vigil, All Saints with Vigil, and Clement have been added, being equipped with both Epistle and Gospel; while Sebastian, Agnes and Agatha, Felicitas (Aug. 1) have been omitted. Two additions have been made, equipped with Gospel only, viz. James and The Machabees in place of Felicitas.

(*b*) Aud has added some forty new cases of Saints with their Gospels, against only a quarter of that number newly equipped with Epistles.[a]

---

[a] The MS. has been greatly revised and modified from time to time, so that exact numbers are not calculable. The three omitted in Pal are omitted also here.

80   *The Sanctorale of the Comes*

(*c*) Qt has Epistles newly added only for five Saints-days—Silvester, Purification, Cathedra Petri, John and Paul, Cornelius and Cyprian: it omits none. In general it keeps close to the Standard Epistle-list, except in so far as it adds feasts equipped with a Gospel only.

(*d*) Ver, which is very similar, adds Purification,[a] Cathedra Petri, and Cornelius and Cyprian with the Exaltation of Holy Cross. The Invention of Holy Cross is omitted: the rest are all included, but the Assumption and the Decollation of St. John Baptist have lost their Epistles, and thus have joined the feasts which are provided with Gospel only.

This class of Comes, therefore, keeps fairly close, so far as Epistles are concerned, to the old form of Standard Epistle-list.

§ 2. As a rule, on those feasts which are taken over into the Comes from the Standard series, the Epistles are not changed, but this is not always the case.[b]

§ 3. The new days thus brought into use have Epistles as follows:

Silvester. *Plures facti* (CL *b*). Aud and Qt: also in Qt *Beatus vir q. inventus* CXLVII *b*.
Purification. *Ecce ego mitto* A 25. Pal, Aud.
  In omnibus requiem CXVIII. Qt and Ver.
Cathedra Petri. Petrus Apostolus (1 Pet. i. 1–7) (p. 70). Qt, Ver, Bes.
Annunciation. *Egredietur virga* CXLIV. Aud.
Gervasius and Protasius. *Scimus quoniam* CXLVIII *c*. Aud.
Pope Stephen. *Doctrinis variis* CL *c*. Aud.
Felix and Adauctus. *Benedictus D and P* CLI *e*. Aud.
Vigil of the Assumption. *Sapientia laudabit* CLIV *c*. Pal.
Nativity of the B. V. M. *Ego quasi vitis* A 179. Aud.
Protus and Jacinth. *Lingua sapientium* CLII *a*. Aud.
Cornelius and Cyprian and Exalt. Crucis. *Lingua sapientium* CLII *a*. Pal.
  Expectatio iustorum CLIII *b*. Aud.
  Hoc sentite LXI. Qt, Ver.
Vigil of Matthew. *Beatus homo* CXLVII *a*: and Day *Unicuique* CXLVIII *b*. Pal.

---

[a] It probably added also Silvester; but, as the MS. has lost its early part, this is uncertain.

[b] *e.g.* Qf has *Exurgens* (p. 70) for SS. Philip and James. For Oct Apostolorum there is given *Deus personam* (Gal. ii. 6–10) in Qf and Aud, as in A 147; but *Unicuique* CXLVIII *b* in Bob. For the Assumption *Ego quasi vitis* A 179 in Qt, Bob: for Decollation XVII in Qt but A 161 in Qf.

The Sanctorale of the Comes

Vigil of All Saints. *Et ecce ego J. vidi in* A 189. Pal.
All Saints' Day. *Et ecce . . . vidi alterum* A 190. Pal.
but Vidi turbam (Rev. vii. 9–12) . . . in saec. saeculorum Amen. (*Late hand.*) Aud.
Clement. Itaque fratres mei (Phil. iv. 1–3) . . . in libro vitae. Pal.

§ 4. The second group (Mu, Qf, Pam, Bob) of Comes MSS. are all alike, in that, when they enlarge the Sanctorale, they provide an Epistle (as well as a Gospel) for each addition. But they pursue this common policy in varying ways.

Pam shows comparatively few entries in the Sanctorale that were not in the Standard. Most of the fourteen are familiar members of the Kalendar of the early Gospel-books or familiar additions to it—such as Candlemas and the Nativity of the B.V.M., added in the early stage of enlargement, or else the Apostles—St. Matthew and SS. Simon and Jude added at a later stage; but the addition of Cathedra Petri (CLVIII*a*) in the week of Septuagesima is unusual, and has a Gelasian flavour.[a]

Bob is made to fit the Sanctorale of the *Hadrianum* almost exactly, with the addition of St. Columban at November 23.

Mu and Qf, on the other hand, represent the Sanctorale of a 'Mixed Sacramentary'; indeed, they have already been described so in vol. II, ch. XI, concerning their Gospels.

§ 5. All these Comes MSS., while keeping in the main the traditional Epistles of the lectionaries, and agreeing, therefore, on these days, differ widely from one another in their way of providing Epistles for days which were not included in the old tradition. They draw chiefly upon a common set of passages—in fact, upon the Commune; but they differ in what they draw out of it. Thus, while the old days exhibit uniformity, the new days show divergence.

§ 6. Apart, however, from divergence of usage, there is some small additional material which comes late into use for Epistles through this multiplication of Saints-days, besides what has been noted above as being brought in by the first Comes-group.

George. Omne gaudium (Jas. i. 2–12) . . . diligentibus se. Qf.
Vitalis. Vobis datum (Phil. i. 29–ii. 4) . . . que aliorum. Qf.
Decoll. Predicauimus (1 Thess. ii. 9–20) . . . et gaudium. Bob.

[a] See vol. II, p. 268.

CHAPTER VII

The Gospels of the Comes MSS.

FOR completeness' sake, and to supplement vol. II, we must glance back to the sets of Gospels which are incorporated into the various Comes MSS. The alliance with the Epistles has tended to break up still further the old form of the 'Capitulare Evangeliorum'. The group Pal, Aud, Qt, and Ver, as has been already shown, sacrificed the Gospel-list to the Epistle-list in the Sanctorale, and the same is true in regard to the week-days. But each Comes has its own way of dealing with the situation: it seems to adopt and adapt the particular form of developed Capitulary which it prefers. Thus, while there are some respects in which the Comes MSS. hang together—*e.g.* the beginning of the list with 272—in many of the points of divergence that have come out in the course of the development of the Capitulary they widely differ. As to such familiar points as the number of Sundays after Epiphany, the Lenten Thursdays, the use of the Alternative ferias, the enumeration and number of the weeks in the summer, the place of the summer Embertide, and the like, there is no sort of agreement.

But what is most significant is the fact, that all alike include in more or less degree festivals and other features which are characteristic of the later developments of the Gospel-series.

In short, the Comes, as this group shows it, is both individualistic and relatively late. It shows no sign of being early in date, or of standing at the head of a tradition, no more in its Gospels than in its Epistles. On the contrary, its method is eclectic; and consequently its variety is so great that no attempt can profitably be made to set out the differences in detail. Far from being the source of the tradition, in fact, the emergence of the Comes has tended still further to disintegrate the existing Capitulary.

In general it may be noted that, within this group of four, Qt and Ver lie closer to one another than the rest, and that Aud is specially radical and individual.

A few special particularities are worth notice.

Aud, Pam, and Qf have no Commune.

Pal has drawn its Gospel for XL$^\text{I}$v from the Earlier series *Audistis...non peiurabis...*(Vol. II. pp. 65, 141). It has very few Votives, but includes an Epistle and Gospel for each day in a week on the plan attributed to Alcuin (p. 64).

Aud exhibits a very marked reshuffling of the Sundays and

The Gospels of the Comes MSS.

week-days in the summer season. Thanks to the plan of admitting festivals without providing an Epistle for them, the Sanctorale is unusually large. Still, it omits many Saints-days once included in the capitulary, while nevertheless, it includes late additions. Among the Votives provision is made for three baptismal scrutinies in some G-Bs. Tommasi gives from other MSS. some Epistles for them. At p. 332 for XL³ii, Benedixit Jacob (Gen. xlviii. 15–20), and L *a*: from his MS. O: but in his MS. S. is Effundam (Ezech. xxxvi. 25–9). And for XL⁴iv (p. 334) in S. LIII *a* (to verse 7) and Expoliate vos (Col. iii. 9–16 or 17).

Qt retains the old reckoning in Lent as 'tregesima' and 'vigima', which shows its adherence to the terminology of the lectionary. There is a number of cases of added 'concordia'. At the end of a long set of Votives there is added 'Leguntur IV euangelia initia in aurium apertionem'.[a]

The problem of the relation of the two MSS. (Qt and Ver) would probably repay further investigation. Each bears traces of having possessed an orderly enumeration of the sections, which presumably existed completely in the archetype, but has been only fitfully reproduced in the copies. It is quite different from that which is adopted here from the Corbie Epistle-book, and it must have belonged to a proper Comes. The numbers are most fully given in the earlier and later parts of Ver. They range there from XXXIV at Septuagesima (which agrees with the previous contents as shown in Qt) to CCXII on the day before Advent (Ang⁶iv). Reckoning backwards from CCXII the numbers correspond with those given as far as CLXXVII Lawr², but Timothy has CLXXII. In the earlier part the numbering seems to agree as far as LXXIX, Vig Pasch; but thenceforward the numbers cease till CLXXII appears, and then the numbering seems to be in excess of the entries. No explanation is available. In any case, however, the existence of the enumeration suggests that the archetype was a standard document.

It still remains to add a note on the character of the Gospel-lists as found in the second group of Comes MSS. They are more normal than those just described: or else more abnormal: and in either case they can be described summarily.

Pam is a composite text as printed, and not a single MS.; but for this purpose the variants which Pamelius had before him do not seem to be important. The compiler of the Comes of St. Donatien of Bruges (which apparently is the main authority for Pamel's

---

[a] As in Tommasi, v. 451. See also Mabillon's *Ordo Romanus*, vii, § 4, in *P.L.* lxxviii. 996.

text) utilized a familiar type of the Standard Gospel-list in its later form, when the series of Sundays in Summer had already been brought into its present form, and when the Alternative Series for week-days had taken the place of the Standard set. The Lenten Thursdays, except XL²v, have the Johannine Gospels.

But there are many signs that the Epistle-list has dominated its partner. At the fifth week after Epiphany there are features common to the Comes books, but different from the Standard Gospels. The Saints-days are few and they seem to be determined mainly by the Epistle-list. Specially noticeable are Cathedra Petri in January and S. Felicitas on August 1.

There is no 'Commune'; and the Votives are very few, being confined to Dedication Festival **284**, the Ordination Services, and the 'Agenda mortuorum'. Nos. **193, 7** and **119** are brought in for the Consecration of Bishops and also *Designauit* (Lu. x. 1–7), which is not in the Standard series.

Bob, on the other hand, has a list of Gospels which seems to be modelled not on any lectionary but on the 'Hadrianum' Sacramentary, at least, so far as its Sanctorale is concerned. It makes very small use of the Alternative ferias, but it rearranges those of the Standard series, utilizing **34, 36** at Septuagesima and **37, 23** at Sexagesima. The distribution of the Saints-days among the weeks is also rearranged.

There is a Commune of the usual fifteen basic entries (Nos. I–XIII, XIX, XX, of vol. II, p. 107), and reference is made to it from elsewhere. The set of Votives is short and incomplete.

The two other MSS. of this group (Mu and Qf) have already been considered, so far as their Gospels are concerned, in vol. II, chapter XI, among MSS. which exhibit marked Gelasian influence.

CHAPTER VIII

Theotinchus

IN an appendix to the *Capitularia*[a] Baluze printed at vol. II, 1309 a Comes derived from a MS. from Beauvais. The preface to it begins thus:

> In Christi nomine anni circuli liber comitis incipit, auctus a Theotincho indigno presbytero rogatu viri venerabilis Hechiardi Comitis Ambianensis. . . .

[a] (Paris, 1677.) The outline is given also by Ranke in his Appendix V.

This Comes is interesting as being a private venture compiled by Theotinchus at Hechiard's request, working on the old material of a 'mixed' Lectionary, following the Alcuinian Comes in the later part; and all through supplementing so as to provide for a daily mass. The method adopted will be seen from the following analysis of the early part of the document.

Up to Innocents' day all is according to the Standard, the Epistles being I–VII, and the Gospels **272**, **1–6**. If December 29 is a Sunday, it is to have Epistle IX with the Gospel *Erat Joseph*, but if it is a week-day the Epistle is to be Gen. ii. 7–14 and the Gospel *Venit Jesus* = Ep^1w. On the 30th the reading from Genesis is continued (ii. 15–19) and the Gospel is Ep^1f; St. Silvester follows with Epistle CL*b* and Gospel *Vigilate* = **7**; and Oct dom. has II and **8**. At Jan. 1 begin 'lectiones ex libri comitis'.

Jan. 2 has Genesis ii. 20–iii. 7 with *Circuibat* Ep^3f.

Jan. 3. St. Genoveva with a new lesson from Wisdom, and *Audistis*. (Mt. v. 27–42.)

Jan. 4 has Dan. i. 1–15, and **261**.

Jan. 5 has Genesis iii. 7–19 and Mt. xiii. 13–16, as well as III and **9** for the Vigil. After a normal Theophany, the selector turns to Isaiah, and takes five lessons thence, with Gospels from St. Mark, but registers St. Lucian of Beauvais at Jan. 8 with Wisdom vi. 2–11 and *Sicut fulgur*, a rare gospel.

The octave of the Epiphany follows, with Epistle XIII and Gospel **13**. Theoph¹ is normal with XII and **11**.

The week following is mainly occupied with saints—Felix, Marcellus, Sulpicius, Prisca, Mary and Martha, Fabian and Sebastian, Agnes, Vincent, fitted with lessons taken from the succeeding chapters of Genesis and new passages from Wisdom vii and xi. The only feria is Jan. 15, which has a lesson of the set from Genesis, and a rare Gospel, Mk. x. 46–52. The Gospels of the Saints-days are more conservative, but for some new saints new ventures are made.

The next week is similarly treated. The saints are Macharius and Emerentianus† (Jan. 23), Proiectus (Jan. 25), and Agnes. Gospels **18, 19, 20** are fitted in on the 25th, 26th, and 27th, and **35** appears for St. Agnes on the 28th.

The third week has Genesis for ferias, and indeed, they continue up to Septuagesima. The Saints-days are Brigida on Feb. 1, with Candlemas and Agatha. The Gospels are generally allotted in a mechanical way, **22, 23, 29, 31, 32**, to the ferias, not as in the older Comes.

The fourth week is similar. It is distinguished by having the

Nativity of St. Thomas on Feb. 8,[a] and Zoticus Irenaeus Hyacinth Amantius and Soter on Feb. 10.

A fifth week follows with these Saints-days: Valentine Vitalis Felicula and Zeno on Feb. 14; Onesimus and Juliana on Feb. 16; 'Polychronius episc.' on Feb. 17.

Septuagesima comes between Feb. 20 and 21. Cathedra Petri on the 23rd interrupts the series of lessons from Genesis, but its Gospel is one of a series from St. Luke, which extends from Feb. 1 to Lent. Before Quinquagesima there comes on March 7 Perpetua and Felicitas. The entries up to Lent have been numbered 1–67 continuously more or less. This numbering is resumed after Low Sunday, but the chief Saints-days as well as the Sundays are usually left unnumbered, and Whit-week is excluded too from the enumeration. With Lent and Easter-week we return to the normal: indeed, we read at XL[1] 'Hic plenarius sequitur ordo sicut in libro comite continetur usque octabas paschae.'[b] But it is noteworthy that before Oct Pasch comes the Annunciation, dated, but called 'In conceptione S. Mariae' with CXLIII a and **54**.[c]

After Low Sunday there begins a series of ferial lessons from the Acts, and later the Sapiential books are used increasingly to fill vacant places. Some attention is paid on Sundays and the older Saints-day to the plan of the Standard, and some to the provision of the Alternative Series, but innovation is more prominent than conservatism. A series of ferial lessons from the Apocalypse begins at cap. 107 after Pent[3], and extends to cap. 136 at the end of the week of Apost[5], when Ecclesiasticus comes in again. It is succeeded by another from Hebrews extending from cap. 149 to 186. Whitsuntide is fairly normal, but at the Vigil a ferial Epistle and Gospel are provided as well as the usual lessons of the Vigil.

During the Summer-time the Sundays begin with Pent[1-6] and familiar lessons, but then there comes trouble. The compiler now inclines to follow Alc, but a later hand has altered things, so that the Sundays run thus:

Apost[1,2] are omitted, but the enumeration shows no break:

Apost[3] is not so numbered, and it has no Epistle; the Gospel is **174** of Apost[3]. Thenceforward while the Gospels run on normally with those of Apost[4-6], Lawr[1-5], and Cypr[1-4]: the corresponding Epistles run thus:

---

[a] See vol. I. 39.

[b] The Sundays in Lent are called by the old names Dom. II. XXX[a], Dom. XX[a]. On the Thursdays the Epistles are normal; the Gospels, except the last, are Johannine.

[c] This, like many other entries, recalls the Gelasian tradition as regards the Saints.

Theotinchus

Apost⁴, Alc 151; Apost⁵, cxi = A 152; Dominica (name erased) Alc 162; Lawr², 163; Lawr³, (erased); Lawr⁴, (erased); Lawr⁵, cxxii = 166; Dominica mensis vi, cxxiii; Dom. mensis viii, cxxv; Dom. mensis vii, cxxix; Dom. mensis vii again, cxxxi; Cypr³, cxxxii.

This half-hearted following of Alc at this point is to be noted (see p. 42). The Summer Embertide follows Pent⁴, and that of September lies between the two Sundays marked Dom. mensis vii.

After Cypr³ comes a gap in the MS. between cap. 186 and cap. 218. The next Sunday extant is Nativ⁻² followed by the Embertide, Nativ⁻¹ and Vigil. Domini ad nonam (111 *a* and **272**).

Apart from the originality of this way of handling the old material, the chief interest in the second half, as in the first[a], lies in the Saints-days. Gelasian influence is again noticeable, as in the earlier half of the year. The rest is as follows:

April 11. Nat. S. Leonis papae.
      14. ,, SS. Tiburtii Valeriani & Maximi.
      24. ,, S. Georgii mr.
      27†. ,, S. Richarii cf. in Centulo.
      29†. ,, S. Theodorae vg. et S. Vitalis.
May 1. ,, SS. Philippi et Jacobi. Ambianis Accii et Accioli.
      3. Inv. S. Crucis.
      6. Nat. S. Matthaei ap.
      7. ,, SS. Alexandri Eventi et Theodoli.
      (10). Romae Nat. S. Gordiani.
      12. ,, ,, SS. Nerei et Achillei; Pancratii mr. et Soteris vg. cum aliis dciii.
      13. Trijecto Dep. S. Servatii ep. and cf.
      14. Nat. S. Cyriaci mr. et cccciv qui cum eo passi sunt Mediolanis.

[a] They comprise there:
Dec. 31. Silvester.
Jan. 3. Genoveva.
    8. Lucian. (Belloacus.)
   14. Felix.
   16. Marcellus.
   17. Sulpicius.
   18. Prisca.
   19. Maria† and Martna.
   20. Fabian and Sebastian.
   21. Agnes.
   22. Vincent.
   23. Macharius and Emerentianus.
   25. Projectus.
Jan. 28. Agnes, de natiuitate.
Feb. 1. Brigida.
   2. Purif. B. V. M.
   5. Agatha.
   8. Natl. St. Thomae.
  10. Zoticus Ereneus Jacinctus Amantius and Soter.
  14. Valentine Vitalis Felicula and Zeno.
  16. Onesimus Juliana.
  17. Polycronius.
  23. Cath. Petri.
Mar. 7. Perpetua and Felicitas.
  25. In conceptione S. Mariae.

88 *Theotinchus*

After Pentecost.

May 19. Nat. S. Pudentianae.
20. Romae Nat. SS. Gervasii et Protasii.
22. In Corsica passio S. Iulianae vg.
25. Nat. S. Urbani ep. et cf.
28. Parisius dep. S. Germani ep. et cf., et trsl. corporis S. Gentiani mr. Ambianensium.
29. Treveris dep. S. Maximi ep.
30. Nat. S. Petronillae.

June 2. Romae Nat. SS. Marcellini et Petri exorcistae cum aliis XLII.
3. Aurelianis Dep. S. Liphardi presb.
9. Nat. SS. Primi et Feliciani.
12. In Nat. S. Basilidis Naboris et Nazari.
14. In Nat. S. Feliculae.
18. Nat. SS. Marci et Marcelliani, et S. Marinae vg.
19. Nat. SS. Gervasii et Protasi. Nazari et Celsi pueri.
23. Vig. S. Johannis Bapt.[a]
24. Item in die.[a]
25. Vig. Johannis et Pauli.[a]
28. Vig. Apost. Petri et Pauli.
29. Item in die.   Ipso die Vig. S. Pauli.
(30). Item in die.

* * * * * *

July 15. Nat. S. Cyriaci.
18. Metis Dep. S. Arnulfi cf.
21. Nat. S. Praxedis.
23. „ S. Apollinaris.
25. „ S. Jacobi ap. Christophori mr. Et Ambianis trsl. S. Firmini.
29. „ S. Felicis Simplicii Faustini et Beatricis.
Tricas Dep. S. Lupi ep. et cf.
30. Nat. SS. Abdon et Sennes.

Aug. 1. Passio Machabeorum septem fratrum et S. Felicitatis sub. Antic.
2. Romae Nat. S. Stephani pont.
6. „ „ S. Xristi†, Felicissimi et Acapiti.
8. „ „ S. Cyriaci.
9. Vig. S. Laurentii.
(10). Item in die.
11. Romae Nat. SS. Tiburtii Valeriani Ceciliae Susannae Cassiani. Et Cameraco Dep. S. Gaugerici.

[a] Misplaced.

Theotinchus

Aug. 12. Nat. S. Eupoli.
  13. „ S. Ypolyti.
  14. „ S. Eusebii.
  15. Adsumptio S. Mariae matris domini.
  16. Nat. S. Leudegarii.
  18. „ S. Agapiti.
  19. Apparitio S. Crucis. Et Nat. S. Andreae Magistri militum.
  20. In Geumatica Nat. S. Philiberti.
  22. Nat. S. Timothei.
  24. In India Nat. S. Bartholomaei apost. Rome S. Aureae vg. Et Dep. S. Audoeni ep. et cf.
  25. Arelato Nat. S. Genesi mr.
  28. Romae Nat. S. Hermetis. Africa Dep. S. Agustini.
  29. In Campania Nat. S. Sabinae vg. Et passio S. Johannis Bapt.
  30. Item in S. Johannis.
Sept. 1. Ambianis Dep. S. Firmini ep. & cf.
  5. In Gallia ciuitate Vensuntio Nat. SS. Ferioli et Ferutioni cum sociis eorum.
  8. Nativ. S. Mariae dei genitricis. Et nat. S. Adriani mr.
  9. Dep. S. Audomari ep. & cf.
  10. „ S. Hilarii, ep.
  11. Nat. SS. Proti et Iacincti.
  13. Turonis Dep. S. Lidoris ep. Et Andigavis Dep. Maurilionis ep.
  14. Nat. S. Cornelii pont. et S. Cypriani atque Exalt. S. Crucis. Item de cruce.
  15. Nat. S. Nicomedis.
  16. „ SS. Virg. Luciae et Eufemiae.
  17. In Ledio Dep. S. Landiberti ep.
  20. Nat. SS. Dorondoni Dorothei Privati Felicis Constantiae qui passi sunt sub Nerone.
  21. In Persida Nat. S. Matthaei ap. et evang. Et S. Lucae evang.
  22. Agauno Nat. SS. Maurici Exsuperi Candidi cum aliis quinque millia DCLXXXV.
  23. Nat. S. Teclae vg. et S. Marci evang.
  24. „ S. Johannis Baptistae et SS. Juliani Christophori.
  25. In Gallia Ambianis Nat. S. Firmini mr.
Nov. 8.* Nat. SS.* Quatuor coronatorum et* S. Ragnulfi mr.*
  9. Passio S. Theodori mr.

Nov. 10. Romae Dep. S. Leonis ep. et S. Mennae.
   11. Turonis Dep. S. Martini ep. & cf. In. vig.
  [12.] Item in die.
   13. Nat. S. Bricii.

After this the enumeration ends; the Embertide follows, Vig Nativ⁻¹ and Nativ. Then come the Saints-day entries of the last half of November and all December (unnumbered).

Nov. 16. Gallia Dep. S. Eucherii ep.
   17. Dep. S. Aniani ep. & cf. Aurilianis.
   22. Nat. S. Caeciliae vg. Valeriani Tiburcii et Maximi mr.
   23. „ S. Clementis et S. Felicitatis et S. Columbani.
   24. „ S. Chrisogoni.
   29. „ S. Saturnini.
   30. „ S. Andreae In vig. In die. Et eodem die S. Ambrosii.
Dec. 1. Dep. S. Elegi.
   10. Romae Dep. S. Damasi papae.
   11. Nat. S. Eulaliae vg. et SS. mrr. Victorici Fusciani et Gentiani.
   12. Dep. S. Walerici cf.
   13. „ S. Autberti ep. Camaracum Et S. Luciae vg.
   18. Nat. S. Afrae vg.
   21. Romae Dep. S. Innocentii ep.
   22. Romae inter duos lauros Nat. SS. triginta martyrum.
   23. In Nicomedia Nat. SS. DCCCLX mr.
   24. Cappadocia Nat. quadraginta virginum.

The Saints-days show clearly that a Gelasian influence has affected not only the early part of the year. Many of the entries in the later part recall the old Hieronymian Martiloge, and some carry back to Rome and the Catacombs.

The chief area of local interest is, however, Northern France: the places quoted include St. Riquier, Maestricht, Amiens, Paris, Trier, Orleans, Metz, Troyes, Cambrai, Jumièges, Besançon, Tours, Liège; and Amiens is especially well represented. The bulk of the Frankish Saints belong to the 7th century.

A short set of Votives follows, drawn for the most part from familiar sources, mainly from the Standard lists, but some from Alc. This is followed by the nine lessons of the Vigils of the Dead.

We are left with several interesting and unsolved problems:
  1. Who was this Count of Amiens, and of what sort was this chaplain of his—if chaplain he was—who calls to us out of the dark?

Theotinchus 91

2. Does this list imply—as it seems to do—that there was a daily mass in the Count's chapel?
3. And when did they live? The place is plain enough, but the date is elusive.
4. A number, however, of the entries of Saints-days can be explained by Delehaye's Commentary on the *Martyrologium Hieronymianum* in AA. SS. Nov. vol. II, part 2.

CHAPTER IX

Composite Lessons

IN the passages used for the liturgical Gospels, there was little need for any manipulation of the text. A few opening words were prefixed, such as 'In illo tempore', to introduce an event, or 'Dixit Jesus discipulis suis', to introduce a parable or some other saying of the Lord. Similarly, some slight modification was sometimes made at the beginning or the end of the passage in order to secure a satisfactory opening or conclusion. In the body of the Gospel-lesson no change was normally needed or made. Some bringing together of the divergent texts of the Synoptic Gospels is found in the liturgical Gospels, as indeed it is also in the non-liturgical texts of the Gospels; but such a procedure seems to have been little, if at all, used for liturgical purposes.

There was no need therefore to deal with the subject in the previous volume.

In regard to the other lessons read at Mass the case is different, and especially the case of those taken from the Old Testament. In them there are found a considerable number of more or less composite lessons, which are peculiar in their liturgical form to the Lectionaries.

The extent to which various passages have been brought together, or modifications have been made in order to provide a suitable lesson, varies considerably.

First to be noted are the conventional introductions and closes. An Epistle usually opens with 'Fratres' only; but the Pastoral Epistles and the Catholic Epistles have 'Karissime' or 'Karissimi' for the opening. Passages of narrative, whether from the O.T. or the N.T., have 'In diebus illis'; those from prophetic books have 'Haec dicit dominus deus', or the like.

There is, naturally enough, more variety about the endings and less system. If a closing formula is wanted its nature depends on the preceding words: but prophetic lessons can easily end with some such phrase as 'dicit dominus deus noster' or 'vester'. Lessons from Epistles attract such a phrase as 'in Christo Jesu domino nostro'. Where a doxology or a phrase like 'in saecula saeculorum Amen' or 'usque in sempiternum' is suitable, it is always welcomed.[a]

These are but formal affairs: more interesting are lessons which draw their contents from different bits of the same portion or even from different portions, or, more rarely, from different books.[b]

These composite lessons, as might be expected, are mainly drawn from the Old Testament. They are, therefore, found chiefly either (i) at those periods and occasions when an Old Testament Lesson supplements or is substituted for a N.T. Lesson, as in the week-days of Lent or the Ember Seasons, or again at Christmastide, where at the beginning of the year a bit of an older and ampler series of lessons has survived; or (ii) where the Vigil-service has survived, as at Easter Even or the Vigil of Pentecost, with its systematic set of biblical lessons; or (iii) in the Proper or Common of Saints for which the Sapiential books made some much-needed provision; or (iv) where Votive Masses needed a composite or varied passage in order to be suitable for their several purposes.

The extent to which any adaptation within the lesson has been made varies greatly: sometimes only a verse or a phrase is omitted, or a single word is introduced or modified. On the other hand, there are a few lessons made up from many extracts drawn out and welded together either from one chapter or from several passages of the same context, or even from different books.

The composite lessons occurring in the early part of the series give suitable examples, as the following set of them will show.

Composite Lessons in the Early part of the Standard Lectionary

I *a*. (Christmas.)
  Isa. lxii. 1–4. Propter Sion non tacebo ... complacuit domino in te.
II *a. De nocte.*
  Isa. ix. 2. Populus gentium qui ambulabat ... orta est eis.
    6, 7. Paruulus enim natus est nobis ... in sempiternum.

[a] Where any noticeable omission of such endings is made in printing, it is indicated by three or four points.

[b] No. cxxxvii is from Proverbs and Ecclesiasticus: but the Sapiential books were often regarded as a whole.

Composite Lessons

III *a. Mane prima.*
    Isa. lxi. 1–3. Spiritus domini . . . ad glorificandum.
    lxii. 11, 12. Ecce d. auditum fecit . . . redempti a d. Deo n.
IV *a. In die.*
    Isa. lii. 6–9. Propter hoc . . . consolatus est d. populum suum.
         10. Et videbunt . . . salutare dei nostri.
V. *St. Stephen.*
    Acts vi. 8–10. Stephanus plenus . . . loquebatur.
       vii. 54–60. Audientes autem . . . obdormiuit in d.
VI. *St. John.*
    Ecclus. xv. 1, 2. Qui timet deum . . . honorificata.
         3.[a] Cibabit eum . . . hereditabit illum d. D. n.
XIII. *Oct Theoph.*
    Isa. xxv. 1. Domine deus meus honorificabo te, laudem tribuam nomini tuo, qui facis mirabiles res.
         Consilium tuum antiquum verum fiat.
    xxvi. 11. Domine excelsum est brachium tuum.[b]
    xxviii. 5. Coronata est gloriae.
    xxxv. 1, 2. Exultet desertum exultent solitudines Jordanis; et populus meus videbit altitudinem domini maiestatem dei.
        10. Et erit congregatus redemptus per D.: et veniens in Sion cum laetitia: et laetitia sempiterna erit super caput eius, laus et exultatio.
    xli. 18. Et aperiam in montibus flumina et in mediis campis fontes disrumpam et terram sitientem sine aqua confundam.
    lii. 13. Ecce puer meus exaltabitur, eleuabitur et sublimis erit valde.
    xii. 3–5. Haurietis aquas . . . in uniuersa terra d. d. O.

I *a* and II *a* are made up of selected verses taken from a single passage: in III *a* the arrangement cuts across the familiar division into chapters. In VI six words are omitted, and in IV *a* only four. When we reach XIII we are faced with a lesson made up of nine different extracts from Isaiah. At XVI we have the first case of a liturgical adaptation affecting the N.T. In this epistle after 'non concupisces' are added the words 'rem proximi tui'. At XXIV there is an addition at the close 'quia misericors sum d. D. tuus'.

The Embertide lessons at XXXII exhibit several specimens. At XXXII *a* two words are added: at XXXII *c* an adapted form of verse 23 introduces verses 2–5: in XXXII *e* there is a form of the Song of the Three Children.

Let these early specimens suffice. For the rest it will be mainly sufficient to give a bare list of the chief places where a composite lesson is to be found—XXXVI, XLIV, XLV, XLVI, LVII, LVIII, LXII*a*, LXVI*b, *g*. But in Eastertide, when the 'Acts' is being read, there

    [a] Old Latin Version: see Sabatier, *Versiones*, ii. 556–83.
    [b] *Add* Deus Sabaoth.

are modifications and combinations of passages even from a N.T. book—LXX, LXXI, LXXXVIII, which are thus *sui generis*.

The Summer Embertide—XCVII, XCVIII, and XCVIII* a, b, c—brings us back to the O.T., and so does that of September, CXXVI, CXXVI a, and CXXVIII c, d. Otherwise, after a single exception at CVII for St. Paul's day there is nothing more that is noticeable until we reach some passages required for particular Saints-days, CXVI at St. Lawrence, CXVIII at the Assumption, CXX at the Decollation of St. John Baptist, CXXXVII at St. Andrew.

But at the Commune, from CL onwards, there is much use of composite lessons, drawn in the main from O.T. books, especially the Sapiential literature.

The following are to be noted:

CL a is made up of eight or nine detached passages drawn from Ecclus. l, xliv, and xlv.

CLI b, c, and f are all composite; the last is one of the rare cases where the art of compounding has been applied to a N.T. book (2 Tim. ii. 8–10; iii. 10–12).

CLII a has verses from Prov. xv.

CLII b has verses from Sap. v.[a]

CLIII b takes verses from Prov. x and xi.

CLIV a = CXVI.

CLIV c has five verses from the beginning of Ecclus. xxii, with bits of verses 21, 22.

CLIV d combines Sap. vii. 30 with viii. 1–4.

The provision of Epistles for the Votive masses set a hard task to the compiler. He consequently dealt very freely with the Pastoral Epistles in CLV and CLVII a, b, concerning ordinations. A passage from Tobias needed some manipulation to fit it for the Anniversary of a Pope, and even Leviticus needed some handling for the same purpose, CLVIII a, b. The next puzzles are set by wartime at CLXIV and CLXV, but Hezekiah provides some solutions: and thereafter Jeremiah and the Lamentations are very helpful in several problems, as the Schedule of Lessons shows. The Carolingian reforms in judicial and other administration are anticipated in CLXIX–CLXXI, but suitable Scriptures are more easily found in this connexion. Finally, a masterpiece of patchwork closes the list of composite lessons and deserves detailed quotation.

CLXXIII. Ad missam votiuam.

---

[a] In CLII c the verses 1 Pet. i. 3–7 are sometimes combined with CLII d; 1 Pet. iv. 1–2; perhaps originally by a mistake.

Composite Lessons

Isa. xviii. 7. In illa die deferetur munus domino exercituum
xix. 4. et rex fortis dominabitur eorum.
18. In die illa erunt quinque ciuitates
21. et cognoscetur d. . . . et colent eum in hostiis . . . et soluent.
22. Et reuertentur ad d. et placabitur eis et sanabit eos.
24. In die illa erit Israhel benedictio in medio terrae
25. cui benedixit . . . Benedictus populus meus—et opus manuum mearum—et haereditas mea Israhel.

There are further composite lessons to be seen in We and Alc, as well as among the later additions, but there is no need to describe them.

The composite lesson is due to the attempt to provide one which has special reference to some occasion. The opposite impulse is the one which produces 'continuous reading', where the plan is to carry on what has been read previously. There was very little of this tendency at all conspicuously shown in the Gospel-series, for that is dominated by the idea of providing appropriate lessons.

It is otherwise with the Epistle-list. There is far more trace preserved here of the old fashion of continuous reading, such as emerges clearly enough from the homilies of St. Augustine and other early preachers. The analysis in Chapter IV has revealed a measure of 'continuity' which might otherwise be unnoticed, and there are clearer instances in the time after Epiphany. There is a certain continuity about the O.T. lessons of Lent; but it is a continuity of idea—'fasting, weeping and mourning'—not a continuity of books or passages. In some places there seems to be a designed correspondence between the Lesson and the Gospel, but the reasons which determined the choice of the Gospel are in most cases hard to recover,[a] and the correspondences intended are often more conjectural than clear.

[a] See vol. II, p. 87.

INDEXES

INDEX OF SOURCES

pp. 49, 50, 67–73.

Baluze, S., in his *Capitularia* Theo. Comes Theotinchi	. .	84–91	
BESANÇON			
Mu. MS. 184 .	. . .	. 72	
Bes, *see* ROME	. . .	. 69	
Bob, *see* MILAN	. . .	. 73	
CAMBRIDGE			
Fi. (Fitzwilliam Museum)	. .	68	
C. (Sir S. Cockerell) .	. .	70	
CHARTRES			
Aud. MS. 24 .	. . .	. 71	
Corbie, *see* LENINGRAD .	.	26, 49	
Freising, *see* MUNICH	. .	. 45	
LEIPSIG			
Stadtbibliothek MS. cxc	. .	68	
LENINGRAD			
Corbie Q. v.i. No. 16.	.	. 25–7	
MAINZ			
Mz. Domschatz	.	. 68	
MILAN (Ambrosian Library)			
Bob. MS. C. 228 inf.	. .	. 73	
MUNICH			
Freising. MS. 6424	. .	. 45	
MS. MS. 14452	. . .	. 73	

OXFORD (Bodleian Library)
  Bml. MS. 19413 . . . 71
Pam. Pamelius, J., *Liturgicon* . . 72
PARIS (Bibliothèque Nationale)
  Qt. 9451 71
  Alc. 9452 . . 28, 40–4, 67
  Qf. N.A. 1541 72
ROME (Vatican Library)
  TP. Pal. 497 69
  Pal. Pal. 510 71
  TQ. Pal. 44 73
  Bes. MS. Borgia 359 . . 69
ROME (Vallicellana)
  Val. Vallicell. C. 10 . . . 68
Theo, *see* Baluze . . . 84–91
Tommasi, *Opera* (ed. Vezzosi. Rome, 1750)
  for TP and TQ, *see* ROME . 69, 73
  for MS. O and MS. S., *see* . . 83
VERONA (Chapter Library)
  Ver. MS. lxxxii . . . 72
WÜRZBURG (University)
  We. Mp. th. fol. 62 . . 25–8, 67

INDEX OF PERSONS, SUBJECTS, AND BIBLIOGRAPHY

Agimund, *Homiliary*, 30.
Alan of Farfa, *Homiliary*, 76.
Albinus, *see* Alcuin.
Alcuin, 25, 28, 40–6.
Analecta Maredsolana, 74.
Audrad, 71.
Augustine, St., 95.

Baluze, S., *Capitularia* (Paris, 1677), 50, 84.
Baptismal Gospels, 71, 83.
Becker (G.), *Catalogi Bibliothecarum Antiqui* (Bonn, 1885), 45, 79.
Berno of Reichenau, 74.
Bernold of Konstanz, 74.
Bishop, E., *Liturgica Historica* (Oxford, 1918), 45.
Boniface IV, 27.
Boretius: *Mon. Germ. Hist., Capitularia*, 45, 78.
Brinktrine, J., *Sacr. Rossianum* (Freiburg, 1930), 53.

Index of Persons, Subjects, and Bibliography

Capitularia, 45, 50, 84.
Charlemagne, 28, 45.
Chifflet, F., 74.
Cockerell, Sir S., 70.
Comes, 37, 45, 46, 49, 50–61, 65, 68, 73–84.
Commune, 20, 29, 32, 33, 37, 39, 40, 44, 51, 61–3, 68, 71, 84.
Constantius, Bishop, 26, 28, 69, 71, 74–9.

Damasus (Pope), 76, 80.
D'Achery: *Spicilegium* (Paris, 1723), 74.
Delehaye, H., *Martyrologium Hieronymianum*, 91.
Duchesne: *Charta Cornutiana* in *Liber Pontificalis*, 73.

Gattula: *Hist. Abb. Cassin.* (Venice, 1733), 49.
Gospels, 38, 81–4.
Gregory (St.), 48, 80.

Hechiard, 84, 85.
Helisachar, 45, 46.
Hittorp (M.), 72.

Jahrbuch für Liturgie-Wissenschaft, 71.
Jerome (Pseudo-), 26, 46, 69, 71, 74–9.
Jerome (St.), 26, 74–9.

Mabillon: on the *Ordo Romanus*, 83.
Manuscripts and Sources, 67–73.
Micrologus, 74.
Monumenta Germaniae Historica, 45, 46.
Morin (Dom): *Revue Bénédictine*, 25, 27, 45, 74, 76.
  Liber comicus, 74.

Ordo Romanus, (in Mabillon, *Mus. Italicum*, and *P.L.* LXXVIII), 53, 70, 83.

Pamelius: *Liturgicon Ecclesiae Latinae*, 50, 72, 83.
Paul the Deacon, 45.

Ralph of Tongres, 72.
Ranke, E., *Das kirchliche Perikopensystem*, 45, 84.
Revue Bénédictine (see Morin: Wilmart).
Römische Quartalschrift, 1929, 30.

Sacramentaries, 53.
  Gelasian, 39, 45, 53, 81, 86, 87, 90.
  Gregorian, 45, 46.
  Hadrian, 46, 50, 53, 73, 84
  Leonine, 29, 37.
  Mixed, 50, 53.
  Paduan, 53.
  Rossianum, 53.
Sanctorale, 37, 65–7, 69, 79–81, 87.
Sigebert's Chronicle, 74.
Smaragdus, *Collectiones*, 77.
Summer, Sundays in, 42–4, 54, 55, 86.
Staerk (Dom A.): *Les MSS. Latins* (1910), 25, 26.
Stations, 1–13, 17, 19, 26, 27, 30, 41, 70.

Index of Persons, Subjects, and Bibliography 99

Temporale, 51.
Theotinchus, 50, 84, 85-90.
Tommasi, *Opera Omnia* (ed. Vezzosi), (Rome, 1750), 28, 32, 45, 63, 69, 70, 73, 74.

Unappropriated lessons, 33-7, 44, 56.

Vacat Sundays, 29-31, 33, 35, 36, 58.

Wilmart (Dom), 71, 72.

INDEX OF PLACES

Africa, 89.
Agaunum (St. Maurice), 89.
Amiens (Ambianis), 84, 87, 88, 89, 90.
Andegavis (Angers), 89.
Antioch, 70.
Arelato (Arles), 89.
Aurelian (Orleans), 88.

Beauvais, 84, 85.
Besançon, 69, 72, 89.
Bobbio, 73, 84.
Bruges, 72, 83.

Cambrai, 89, 90.
Cambridge, 68, 70.
Cameraco (Cambrai), 89, 90.
Campania, 89.
Cappadocia, 90.
Capua, 49.
Centulo, *see* St. Riquier.
Chartres, 50, 67.
Clingen, 78.
Corbie, 25, 39, 48 ff., 63.
Corsica, 88.

Farfa, 76.
Freising, 45.

Gaul, 89, 90.
Geumatica (Jumièges), 89, 90.

India, 89.

Jumièges (Geumatica), 89, 90.

Köln, 72, 78.
Konstanz, 74.

Ledio (Liège), 89, 90.
Leipzig, 68.
Leningrad, 25.
Liège, *see* Ledio, 89, 90.

Maestricht, 87, 90.
Mainz, 69.

Mediolanis, *see* Milan, 73, 87.
Metz, 88.
Milan, 73, 87.
Monte Cassino, 49, 77.
Munich, 45, 73, 76.
Murbach, 50, 72.

Nicomedia, 90.

Orleans, 88, 90.
Oxford, 73.

Paris, 26, 28, 44, 67, 71, 72, 88, 90.
Persia, 89.

Reichenau, 74.
Rome, 87-90.
  Vatican, 32, 68, 69, 71, 73, 74
    see Stations.
  Churches:
    Lateran, 4, 30.
    Pantheon, (S. Maria Martyra), 27.
    St. Cecilia, 70.
    St. Mary Major, 4, 10, 27.
    Twelve Apostles, 30.

St. Gall, 78.
St. Germain des Prés, 26.
St. Pére (Tours), 71.
St. Riquier, 45, 78, 87, 90.
Sens, 71.

Toledo, 74.
Tongres, 72.
Tours, 71, 89, 90.
Trajectus (Maestricht), 87, 90.
Tricas (Troyes), 88, 90.
Trier, 50, 69, 72, 88, 90.
Troyes, *see* Tricas, 88, 90.

Valcassoriana, 68.
Verona, 72.

Würzburg, 25, 27, 67.

INDEX OF ABBREVIATIONS

AA. SS. *Acta Sanctorum* (Bollandist), (in progress).
D.A.C.L. *Dictionnaire d'Archéologie et de Liturgie* (Cabrol and Leclerq), (in progress).
L.P. *Liber Pontificalis* (L. Duchesne).
LXX., LX., L. Septuagesima, Sexagesima, Quinquagesima.
XL. Lent.
P.L. *Patrologia Latina* (Migne).
R.B. *Revue Bénédictine* (in progress).
† indicates a faulty reading.

Superior figures denote the Sunday or the week; ii–vii represent the ferias of any week, whether in XL (Lent) or other seasons, Adv., Nativ., Epiph. or Theoph., Pasch., Pent., Trin., and the like.

INDEX OF LITURGICAL DAYS &c.

Abdon and Sennes, 88.
Accius and Acciolus, 87.
Adrian, 72, 89.
Advent, 31, 32, 38, 51, 59, 60, 78.
Afra, 90.
Agapitus, 88, 89.
Agatha, 41, 69, 85, 87.
Agenda, *see* Dead.
Agnes, 41, 69, 85, 87.
Agnes and Agatha, 3, 26, 29, 39, 41, 65, 67, 79.
Alexander, Eventius, and Theodolus, 87.
All Saints, and Vigil, 30, 31, 43, 66, 67, 69, 79, 81.
 Sunday, 30, 31, 72, 83.
Amantius, 86, 87.
Ambrose, 90.
Anastasia, 1, 4, 12.
Andrew, *Apostle*, 18, 32, 43, 66, 69, 90.
 Vigil, 18, 40, 43, 66, 90.
Andrew, magister militum, 89.
Anianus, 90.
Antidius, 70.
Apollinaris, 8, 88.
Apostles (All): Vigil, 26.
 (Peter and Paul) Octave, 15, 42, 65, 69, 80.
 Station, 4, 11, 12, 13, 17, 19.
Apostles' days added to Kalendar, 48, 61, 63.
Arnulf, 88.
Ascension, Vigil, 57, 67.
Audoenus, 89.
Audomarus, 89.
Augustine of Hippo, 89.
Aurea, 89.
Autbert and Lucy, 90.

Balbina, 5.
Baptism, 30, 71, 83.
Bartholomew, *Apostle*, 16, 25, 48, 66, 89.
Basilides et soc., 69, 88.
Beatrice, 88.
Benedict, 26, 69.
Benignus, 70.
Bricius, 90.
Brigida, 85, 87.

Candidus, 89.
Cassian, 72, 88.
Cecilia, 5, 26, 43, 69, 88.
Celsus, 88.
Christmas, Vigil, 29, 32, 40, 72, 83.
 day, 29, 38, 40, 51.
 octave, 29, 51, 85.
 season, 29, 36, 38, 40.
Christopher, 88, 89.
Chrysogonus, 7, 90.
Clement, 5, 43, 69, 79, 81.
Columban, 73, 81, 90.
Constantia, 89.
Cornelius and Cyprian, 42, 66, 67, 69, 79, 80, 89.
Cosmas and Damian, 63, 69.
Cross (Holy), Apparition, 89.
 Invention, 11, 26, 30, 39, 65, 67, 80.
 Exaltation, 16, 39, 48, 66, 69, 80, 89.
Cyprian, 54, 55; *and see* Cornelius.
Cyriac et soc., 8, 69, 88.

Damasus, 90.
Dead (Agenda mortuorum), 26, 27, 44, 63, 64.
Dedication, 32, 33, 68, 71, 84.
Dominica indulgentia, 38.

Index of Liturgical Days 101

Donatian, 72, 83.
Dorymedon, Dorotheus, et soc., 89.

Easter, 30, 36.
 Octave, 30.
 Even, 30, 38, 41, 46, 48, 52, 53, 70.
Eight hundred and sixty Martyrs of Nicomedia, 90.
Eligius, 90.
Embertide, 29, 31, 35, 38, 42, 48, 53, 55, 72, 81, 90.
Epiphany, Vigil, 29, 40, 52.
 Feast, 29, 37, 38, 40, 85.
 Octave, 52, 85.
Eucherius, 90.
Eulalia, Victor, Fuscianus, and Gentianus, 90.
Eupolus, 89.
Eusebius, 7, 69, 89.
Eutychius, 68, 69.
Exuperius, 89.

Fabian, 69.
Fabian and Sebastian, 85, 87.
Faustinus, 88.
Felicissimus, 88.
Felicitas, 15, 31, 33, 65, 79, 84, 88, 90.
Felicula, 86-8.
Felix, 41, 69, 85, 87.
Felix, 89.
Felix and Adauctus, 80.
Felix, Simplicius, Faustina, and Beatrice, 88.
Ferial, *see* Week-day.
Ferreol and Ferrution, 70, (June 16), 89, (Sept. 5).
Firminius, 88, 89.
Forty Virgins of Cappadocia, 90.

Gaugericus, 89.
Genesius, 89.
Genoveva, 85.
Gentianus, 88.
George, 4, 69, 81, 87.
Germanus of Paris, 88.
Gervasius and Protasius, 42, 80, 88.
Gordianus, 87.
Gregory, 46, 69.

Hermes, 89.
Hilarius, 89.
Hippolytus, 72, 89.
Hippolytus and Cassian, 72.

Indulgentia, Dominica, 38.
Innocent, 90.
Irenæus, 70, 85, 87.

James, *Apostle*, 15, 26, 48, 62, 66, 79, 88.
Jerome, 69.

John and Paul, 4, 12, 31, 42, 66, 69, 80, 88.
 Vigil, 88.
John Baptist, Nativity, 14, 65, 69, 88, 89.
 Vigil, 14, 65, 88.
 Decollation, 16, 26, 42, 66, 67, 69, 80, 81, 89.
John Evangelist, 51, 73.
Julian and Christopher, 89.
Juliana, 86, 87.

Lambert, 89.
Lawrence, 4, 5, 6, 7, 10, 15, 32, 42, 54, 55, 66, 69, 88.
 Vigil, 15, 66, 71, 88.
Lent, 27, 30, 37, 38, 41, 42, 44, 52, 73, 78, 81, 84, 86.
 Palm Sunday, 38, 70.
 Maundy Thursday, 30, 38.
Leo, 87, 90.
Leudegarius, 89.
Lidoris, 89.
Liphard, 88.
Litania maior, 11, 30, 38, 41, 54, 69, 72; *see also* Rogation-days.
Lucia, 90.
Lucia and Euphemia, 89.
Lucian, 85, 87.
Luke, *Evang.*, 48, 89.
Lupus, 88.

Machabees, 40, 68, 69, 79, 88.
Macharius and Emerentiana, 85, 87.
Marcellinus and Peter, 42, 69, 88.
Marcellus, 8, 41, 85, 87.
Marcus and Marcellianus, 69, 88.
Maria† and Martha, 87.
Marina, 88.
Mark, *Evangelist*, 69, 89.
 Station, 6.
Martin, 43, 69, 90.
 Vigil, 43.
Martina, 68, 69.
Mary, B. V.
 Purification, 26, 39, 41, 66, 69, 79, 80, 85, 87.
 Annunciation, 39, 41, 69, 80, 87.
 Dedication S. M. ad Martyres, 27.
 Assumption, 16, 26, 39, 42, 66, 69, 80, 89.
 Vigil, 26, 66, 69, 79, 80.
 Major, 4, 12, 13, 17, 19, 26, 27.
 Nativity, 16, 26, 39, 48, 66, 69, 80, 89.
Matthew, *Evang.*, 18, 48, 62, 63, 66-9, 71, 79, 80, 89.
 Vigil, 17, 48, 66, 67, 79, 80.
Matthias, *Apostle*, 70.
Maurice and comp., 26, 89.
Maurilio, 89.

Index of Liturgical Days

Maximin, 72.
Maximus, 88, 90.
Mediana, 30, 38.
Mennas, 90.
Michael *in monte Gargano*, 68, 69.
Michaelmas, 18, 31, 32, 43, 66, 69, 72.
    Octave, 72.

Nabor and Nazarius, 88.
Natale pape, 32.
Nazarius and Celsus, 88.
Nereus and Achilles, 8.
Nereus, Achilles, and Pancras, 69, 87.
Nicomede, 90.

Onesimus and Juliana, 86, 87.
Ordination, 84.

Pancras, *see also* Nereus, &c., 41.
Pascha, *see* Easter.
Pascha annotina, 39, 41, 72.
Paul, *Apostle*, 3, 7, 10, 14, 31, 69, 88.
    Vigil, 14, 39, 66, 88.
Pentecost, *see* Whitsun.
Perpetua and Felicitas, 87.
Peter and Paul, 31, 32, 88.
Peter, 14.
    Vigil, 14, 88.
Peter, *Apostle*, 3, 5, 7, 10–13, 17, 19, 69.
    Cathedra, 26, 70, 80, 81, 84.
    Chains [ad vincula], 4, 39, 69.
Petronilla, 88.
Philibert, 89.
Philip and James, *Apostles*, 11, 41, 65, 69, 80, 87.
Polycronius, 86, 87.
Praeiectus, 85, 87.
Praxedis, 88.
Primus and Felician, 88.
Prisca, 8, 69, 85.
Privatus, 89.
Processus and Martinian, 66, 69.
Protus and Hyacinth, 72, 80, 89.
Pudentiana, 6, 88.

Quatuor Coronati, 7, 69, 89.
Quintin, 70.

Ragnulf, 89.
Richarius, 87.
Rogation-days, 30, 38, 54, 68, 69, 70.

Sabina, 4, 33, 66, 70, 89.
Saturninus, 69, 90.
Scrutinies, 30, 71, 83.
Sebastian, 3, 29, 65, 69, 79.
Septem Fratres, 69.
Servatius, 87.
Silvester, 7, 29, 40, 66, 69, 80, 85.

Simon and Jude, *Apostles*, 18, 48, 63, 66–9, 81.
    Vigil, 18, 48, 66, 67.
Sixtus, 6, 31, 42, 66, 72 (with Hippolytus and Cassian), 88.
Soteris, 86, 87.
Stephen, *Pope*, 80, 88.
Stephen, *Protomartyr*, &c., 8, 13, 65.
Sulpicius, 85, 87.
Sundays, *see also* Advent, Lent.
    After Christmas, 29, 36, 40, 52, 85.
    After Epiphany, 29, 37, 40, 52, 81, 85, 86.
    LXX, 84, 85.
    LX, 85.
    After Easter, 30, 36, 41, 86.
    After Ascension, 41.
    After Pentecost, 31–7, 42, 44, 54, 81, 86.
    After Apostles, 42, 54, 86.
    After Laurence, 42, 43, 54, 86.
    After Cyprian, 54, 86.
    After Michaelmas [post Ang.], 43, 54.
    Before Christmas, 43, 87.
    Before and after Embertide, 54, 87.
    Dominica vacat, 29–31, 33, 35, 36, 58.
    Dominica mensis —, 54, 87.
    Dominica Indulgentia, 38.
    Trinity, 63, 64, 68.
Susanna, 6, 88.

Tecla, 89.
Theodora and Vitalis, 87.
Theodore, 90.
Theophany, *see* Epiphany.
Thirty Martyrs *inter duos lauros*, 90.
Thomas, *Apostle*, 62, 66, 67.
    Nativity, 86, 87.
Tiburtius, Valerian, &c., 87, 88, 90.
Timothy, 89.
Transfiguration and Vigil, 68, 69.
Tricesima, 38.
Trinity Sunday, 63, 64, 68.

Urban, 88.

Vacat Sunday, 29–31, 33–5, 36, 58.
Valentine, 41, 69, 86, 87.
Valerian, 88, 90.
Vicesima, 30, 38.
Victoricus, 90.
Vincent, 69, 85, 87.
Vitalis, 6, 66, 69, 81, 86, 87.
Votives, 32, 33, 43, 51, 63–5, 71, 84.

Walericus, 90.
Wedding, 23, 32; *see* Votives.
Week-days, 38, 44, 51, 64, 65, 68, 71, 73, 81.
Wednesdays, 56–8.

Index of Liturgical Days

Fridays, 58–61.
Whitsun, 38, 39, 41, 52.
Vigil, 30, 38, 41, 48, 52, 53.
Octave, 30, 31, 39, 41, 72.

Widows, 23; see Votives.

Zeno, 86, 87.
Zoticus, Irenæus, &c., 86, 87.

SCHEDULE OF THE LITURGICAL EPISTLES AND LESSONS

Modern biblical references are on the left, indicating the source of the capitula arranged in their biblical order. Lessons of the Standard Series are in thick type, and their numbering is in Roman figures as at pp. 1–24. With them are included other capitula also, viz.:
1. A few included in the Earlier Series, but not in the Standard Series—marked with *We* and an arabic numeral.
2. The capitula which are in Alc but not the Standard—marked A, or AA (appendix), and in italic. See pp. 40–8.
3. All Capitula additional to the foregoing, with a page reference in the outside column. This column also contains additional reference to some usage of the foregoing for unusual purposes. But Theotinchus (Chapter VIII) is not taken into account here.

GEN.

1: 1–2: 2	**In principio creauit** (Sabb. Sancto a: Sabb. Pent. a)	LXVI*, LXXXVI	
5: 31–8: 21	**Noe uero cum** (Sabb. Sancto b)	LXVI*	
22: 1–19	**Temptauit deus Abraham** (Sabb. Sancto c: Sabb. Pent. b)	LXVI*, LXXXVI	
24: 7	**Loquutus est Abraham** (In itinere. a)	CLXXII	
27: 6–39	**Dixit Rebecca filio** (XL² vii)	XXXIX	
37: 6–22	**Audite somnium** (XL² vi)	XXXVIII	
46: 1–4	**Profectusque est Israel** (In itinere. b)	CLXXII	
48: 15–20	Benedixit Iacob (Scrutiny)		83

EXOD.

12: 1–11	**Dixit d. ad Moysen et Aaron** (XL⁶ vi: Sabb. Sanct. k)	LXVI, LXVI*	
14: 24–15: 1	**Factum est in uigilia** *cum carmine cantemus d.* (Sabb. Sanct. d and e: Sabb. Pent. c)	LXVI*, LXXXVI	
20: 12–24	**Haec dicit . . . [Honora patrem]** (XL³ iv)	XLIII	
24: 12–18	**Dixit d. ad Moysen Ascende** (XL¹ iv)	XXIX	
32: 7–14	**Loquutus . . . Discende de monte** (XL⁴ iii)	XLIX	
11–14	Orauit Moyses (Mens. Sept. vii)	*We 150*	31

LEV.

19: 1, 2, 11–19	**Locutus . . . Ego d. deus uester** (XL⁵ iv)	LVII	
23: 9–11, 15–17, 20, 21	**Dixit . . . Loquere filiis** (Pent.³ Mens. Quarti vii. b)	XCVIII*	
27–32	**Locutus est . . . Decimo die** (Pent.¹⁸ Mens. Sept. vii. a)	CXXVIII	
39–43	**Loquutus est . . . Quinto decimo die** (Pent.¹⁸ Mens. Sept. vii. b)	CXXVIII	
26: 3–12	**Dixit . . . Si in preceptis** (Pent.³ Mens. Quarti vii. d)	XCVIII*	

Schedule of the Liturgical Epistles and Lessons

NUMERI
20: 2, 3, 6, 13   Conuenerunt filii Israhel (XL³ vi)   XLV

DEUT.
11: 22–25   Si custodieritis (XL¹ vii. b)   XXXII
26: 1–3, 7–11   Dixit Moyses, Audi Israel (Pent.³   XCVIII*
                 Mens. Quarti vii. c)
    15–19   Respice de sanctuario (XL¹ vii. a)   XXXII
27: 14   ⎫   Pronuntiabunt Leuite ... Faciet   CLVIII
28: 1–10   ⎭   (Nat. pape)
27: 14   ⎫   Pronuntiabunt leuite ... Susci-   We 185
28: 9–12   ⎭   tauit te (Nat. pape)   32
31: 22–30   Scripsit Moyses canticum (Sabb.   LXVI*, LXXXVI
                 Sanct. n: Sabb. Pent. d)
32: 1–4   Adtende caelum et loquar (Sabb.   LXVI*
                 Sanct. o)

II REG.
7: 8–16   Ego tuli te (Nat. pape)   We 186   32
   8–17   Ego tuli te (Aduent. episc. a)   CLXI   32

III REG.
3: 16–28   Venerunt due mulieres (XL⁴ ii)   XLVIII
8: 14–34   Conuertit rex Salomon (Dedic.)   We 213   32, 33, 64
   22   Stetit Salomon   64
17: 8–16   Factus est sermo (XL² iii)   XXXV
    17–24   Egrotauit filius (XL⁴ vi)   LII
19: 3–8   Venit Helias (XL¹ iv)   XXIX a

IV REG.
4: 1–7   Mulier quedam clamabat   XLII
                 (XL³ iii)
   25–28   Venit mulier serupthis (XL⁴ v)   LI
5: 1–15   Naaman princeps (XL³ ii)   XLI
13: 14–21   Helisaeus aegrotabat (XL⁴ 5)   A 64   52
19: 1, 4–7   Cum audisset rex (Letania a)   CLXIV

II ESD.
1: 4–11   Jeiunauit Esdras   We 180   32
   5–11   Orauit Esdras ... Quaeso (XL¹ v)   A 39   52
8: 1–10   Congregatus est omnis (Pent.¹⁸   CXXVI
                 Mens. Sept. iv. a)

TOBIAS
13: 12–19   Benedicens Tobias (Nat. pape. a)   CLVIII

ESTH.
13: 9–11, 15–17 Orauit Hester ad d. (XL² iv)   XXXVI

JOB
14: 13–16   Quis mihi (Mort.)   A 233

PSALMI
40: 1–3   Sicut ceruus (Sabb. Sanct. q: LXVI*, LXXXVI
                 Sabb. Pent. g)

PROV.
3: 13–20   Beatus homo qui inuenit sap.   CXLVII
                 (Vig. apost. a)

Schedule of the Liturgical Epistles and Lessons 105

PROV.
8: 22–35	D. possedit me	66, 71
10: 6 with Ecclus. 44: 26–27 45: 2–4, 6–9	} Benedictio d. (Vig. Andr.) CXXXVII	
10: 28–32 11: 3–6, 8–11	} Expectatio iustorum (Plur. Mart. CXX, CLIII b. Passio Ioh. Bapt.)	
15: 2–4, 6–9	Lingua sapientium (Plur. sanct. a) CLII	
31: 10–31	Mulierem fortem (Felicitas) CXIV. *We 194*	
25–29	Fortitudo et decor	65

CANT.
1: 1–	Osculetur me	69

SAP.
1: 1–7	Dixit Salomon . . . Diligite (Pent.³ XCVII Mens. Quarti iv)	
1: 6, 7	Benignus est	65
2: 12–23	Dixerunt impii Iudei (XL⁶ iii. a) LXIII	
3: 1–8	Iustorum anime (Plur. mart. a) CLIII	
4: 7–11, 13–25	Iustus autem si morte (Unius CLI conf. c)	
5: 1–5	Stabunt iusti (Philippi et Iacobi) LXXVIII	
16, 17	Iusti in perpetuo (Plur. sanct. b) CLII	
6: 11–21	Qui custodierint	26
7: 7–14	Optaui et datus	62
30–8: 4	Sapientia uincit (Virg. d) CLIV	
10: 10–14	Iustum deduxit d. (Unius conf. d) CLI	
17–21	Reddet deus mercedem (Plur. CLIII mart. c)	

ECCLUS.
2: 7–13	Metuentes d. sustinete	63
18–21	Qui timent d.	62
14: 22 15: 3, 4, 6	} Beatus uir qui in sap. (Conf. siue CLI Mart. b)	
15: 1–6	Qui timet d. (Iohn. Evan. Ap.) VI	93
24: 1–5, 21, 22	Sapientia laudabit (Virg. c) CLIV	
11–13 15–20	} In omnibus requiem (Adsumptio CXVIII S. Mariae)	
14–16	Ab initio	65
20–28	Ego quasi myrrha (In Adsumptione S. Mariae)	26
23–31	Ego quasi vitis (In fest. B. Mariae) *A 179*	
42–25: 2	Rigabo hortum	63
31: 8–11	Beatus uir qui inuentus (Vig. CXLVII Apost. b)	
32: 1, &c.	Rectorem te posuit (Votiva regis) *AA 55*	
35: 2	Sacrificium salutare	64
36: 1–10	Miserere nostri (XL¹ vii. d) XXXII	
39: 1–5	Sapientiam omnium ant.	62
6–13	Iustus cor suum tradidit (Vig. CLI conf. siue Mart.)	
43: 33–& 50: to 31	Benedicentes d. exaltate	70
44: 10–15	Hi sunt uiri misericordie (Oct. CIX Apost.)	

106 *Schedule of the Liturgical Epistles and Lessons*

ECCLUS.

44: 16–27 }	Ecce sacerdos magnus (Unius	CL	
45: 3–20 }	Sac. a)		
45: 1–6	Dilectus deo		62
47: 9–13 }	Dedit d. confessionem		62
24: 1–4 }			
51: 1–8, 12	Confitebor tibi (Vig. Laurentii: Virg. a)	CXVI, CLIV	
13–17	D. meus, exaltasti (Nat. Virg. b)	CLIV	

ISAIA

1: 16–19	Lauamini, mundi estote (XL⁴ iv. a)	L	
2: 1–5	Erit in nouissimis (Mens. dec. iv)	CXLIII	
4: 1–6	Apprehendent (Sabb. Sanct. j: Sabb. Pent. e)	LXVI*, LXXXVI	
5: 1–27	Vinea facta est (Sabb. Sanct. k)	LXVI*	
8–26	Vae qui coniungitis (Contra iudices)	CLXX	
7: 10–15	Loquutus est d. ad Achaz (Mens. dec. iv. a)	CXLIII	
9: 2, 6, 7	Populus gentium qui ambulabat (Nativ. dom. a)	II	92
11: 1–5	Egredietur virga (Mens. dec. vi. Annunc. B.M.V.)	CXLIV. *A 28*	
18: 7 with }	In die illa defertur (Ad	CLXXIII	94
19: 4, 19, 21, 22, 24, 25 }	missam votiuam)		
20–22	Clamabunt ad d. (Mens. dec. vii a)	CXLV	
25: 1, &c.	Domine D. meus honorificabo	XIII	93
35: 1–7	Letabitur deserta (Mens. dec. vii. b)	CXLV	
37: 1–7	Cum audisset rex Ezechias (Laetania a)	CLXIV	
15–17, 20–35	Orauit Ezechias (Laetania b)	CLXIV	
16–	Domine exercituum		72
38: 1–6	Egrotauit Ezechias (L v)	XXIII	
40: 9–11	Super montem excelsum (Mens. dec. vii. c)	CXLV	
42: 1–9	Ecce seruus meus (Mens. dec. vii)	*We 167*	31
43: 1–7	Haec dicit d. creans te (Passio Joh. Bapt.)		26
44: 1–3	Audi Iacob (Pent.³ Mens. Quarti. iv. a)	XCVII	
45: 1–8	Hec dicit d. christo meo (Mens. dec. vii. c)	CXLV	
49: 1–3	Audite insulae (Ioh. Bapt.)	CII	
8–15	Tempore placito (XL⁴ vii)	LIII	
50: 5–10	Dixit Esaias, d. Deus aperuit (XL⁶ ii)	LXII	
52: 6–10	Propter hoc sciet (Nativ.)	IV a	92
53: 1–12	Domine quis credidit (XL⁶ iv. a)	LXIV	
54: 17–55: 11	Haec est hereditas (Sabb. Sanct. f)	LXVI*	
55: 1–11	Omnes sitientes (XL⁴ vii. a)	LIII	52, 53, 83
6–11	Quaerite dominum (XL¹ iii)	XXVIII	
58: 1–9	Clama ne cesses (L vi)	XXIV	
6	Hoc est ieiunium		64
9–14	Si abstuleritis (L vii)	XXV	

Schedule of the Liturgical Epistles and Lessons

ISAIA

58: 10–14	Orietur in tenebris (Mort.)		63 TP.
60: 1–6	**Surge inluminare** (Theoph.)	XI	
61: 1–3 }	**Spiritus d. super me** (Nativ.)	III a	92
62: 11, 12 }			
62: 1–4	**Propter Sion non tacebo** (Vig. Nativ.)	I a	92
11–63: 1–7	**Dicite, filie Sion** (XL⁶ iv. a)	LXIV	

JER.

1: 4–10	**Factum est uerbum** (Vig. Ioh. Bapt.)	CI	
2: 1–7	Factum est . . . Surge (In sterilitate)	*We 202*	33
7: 1–7: 42, 12	**Factum est uerbum ad Ieremiam** (XL³ v)	XLIV & *A 73*	52
8: 4. Is. 40: 8	**Numquid qui cadit** (Laetania c)	CLXIV	
9: 4–9	Unusquisque se (Laetania)	*We 200*	33
11: 18–20	**Dixit Ieremias, Domine demonstrasti** (XL⁶ iii)	LXIII	52
14: 7–9	Si iniquitates (Tribulation)	*A 224*	64
19–22	**Numquid proiciens** (In sterilitate)	CLXVI	
17: 5–10	**Maledictus homo** (XL² v: In sterilitate)	XXXVII, CLXVII	
7–10	Beatus uir qui confidit (XL³ v)	*A 57*	52
13–18	**D. Ieremias, Domine Omnes qui**	LIX	
18: 18–23	**Dixerunt impii** (XL⁵ vii)	LX	
22: 3, 4	Facite iudicium (In temp. belli)	*A 221. We 204*	33, 54, 64
23: 5–8	**Ecce dies uenient** (Adv.⁻⁵)	CXXXIX	
28: 4 & 30: 8–11	Conteram iugum (Mens. Sept. vii)	*We 146*	31
31: 6–14	Surgite et ascendamus		52, 70
7–14	Exultate in laetitia Iacob		52
42: 7–12	**Factum . . . uocauit Iohanan** (In die belli. a)	CLXV	

THRENI

2: 19, 20 }	Loquutus est . . . Consurge, lauda (Pro ubertate)	CLXVIII	
3: 54–58 }			
3: 22, 24–6, 31, 32	**Loquutus est . . . Misericordie d.** (In die belli. b)	CLXV	52

BARUCH

3: 9–38	Audi, Israel, mandata (Sabb. Sanct. g: Sabb. Pent. f)	LXVI*, LXXXVI	

EZECH.

18: 1–9	**Factus est sermo** (XL¹ v)	XXX	
20–28	**Anima que peccauerit** (XL¹ vi)	XXXI	
34: 2–14	**Vae pastoribus Israhel** (Contra episcopos)	CLXXI	
11–16	**Ecce ego ipse** (XL¹ ii)	XXVII	
36: 23–28	**Sanctificabo nomen** (XL⁴ iv. 1)	L	
25–29	Effundam super vos		83
37: 1–14	**Et facta est super me** (Sabb. Sanct. h)	LXVI*. *We 212*	
44: 1–4	Conuerti me (Nat. S. Marie)		26

DAN.

3: 1–23	**Nabuchodonosor rex** (Sabb. Sanct. p)	LXVI*	

108 Schedule of the Liturgical Epistles and Lessons

DAN.

3: 35–45	Orauit Danihel dicens (XL⁵ v)	LVIII	
49–55, &c.	Angelus d. descendebat (Mens. Primi, Quarti, Septimi, Decimi vii. e)	XXXII, XCVIII*, CXXVIII, CXLV	
6: 16–23	Principes et satrapae	We 210	33
7: 7, 9, 10, 13, 14	Aspiciebam in visione		60
9: 15–19	Orauit Danihel dicens, Domine d. noster (XL² ii)	XXXIV	
13: 1–62	Erat vir in Babylone (XL³ vii)	XLVI	
14: 28–42	Congregati sunt Babylonii (XL⁵ iii)	LVI	

OSEE

6: 1–6	In tribulatione sua (XL⁶ vi. 1)	LXVI
4: 2–10	Conuertere Israhel (Pent.¹⁸ Mens. Sept. vi)	CXXVII

JOEL

2: 12–19	Conuertimini ad me (L iv)	XXII	
21–26	Noli timere, terra (Serenitas)	A 223	64
23, 24, 26, 27	Exultate filii Sion (Pent.³ vi)	XCVIII	
28–32	Effundam de spiritu meo (Pent.³ Mens. Quarti vii. a)	XCVIII*	

AMOS

9: 13–15	Ecce dies veniunt (Pent.¹⁸ Mens. Sept. iv. a)	CXXVI

JONAS

3: 1–10	Factum est verbum (XL⁵ ii: Sabb. Sanct. m)	LV, LXVI*

MICH.

7: 14, 16, 18, 20	Domine deus noster, pasce (Pent.¹⁸ Mens. Sept. vii. c)	CXXVIII

HAB.

3: 18, 19	Gaudens gaudebo (Sabb. Sanct.)		53

ZACH.

8: 1, 14, 19	Factum est uerbum (Pent.¹⁸ Mens. Sept. vii. d)	CXXVIII	
9: 9–16	Exalta satis (XL⁵ vii)	A 75	52
1: 12–13: 9, &c.	Si bonum est (XL⁶ ii. a)	LXII	

MAL.

2: 4–7	Scietis quia misi (Sacerd.)	A 226	63, 64
3: 1–4	Ecce ego mittam (Purif. B.M.V.)	A 25	26, 59, 66

II MACH.

1: 23 & 2–5	Orationem faciebant (XL¹ vii. c)	XXXII
12: 42–46	Vir fortissimus Iuda (Mort. a)	CLXXV

ACTS

1: 1–11	Primum quidem sermonem (Ascens.)	LXXXIV	
15–26	Exurgens Petrus		70, 80
2: 1–11	Cum complerentur (Pent.)	LXXXVII	

Schedule of the Liturgical Epistles and Lessons 109

ACTS

2: 14–21	**Stans Petrus** (Pent. iv)	XC	
22–28	**Aperiens P. . . . Viri Israhelite** (Pent. vi)	XCII	
3: 1–10	Petrus et Iohannes (Vig. Petri)	CIV	
10: 34 & 3: 12–19	Aperiens Petrus os (Pasch. iv)	LXXI	
4: 24–43	Leuauerunt vocem (Vig. Apost.)		26
32–35	Multitudinis autem (Vig. Asc.)	LXXXIII	
5: 12–16	Per manus apostolorum (Pent. iv. a)	XC	
17–21	Exurgens autem princeps (Philip & J.)	*A 105*	
29–42	**Respiciens autem Petrus** (Oct. Pent. a)	XCIV	
6: 8–10 \} 7: 54–60 \}	**Stephanus plenus gratia** (Nat. Steph.)	V	93
8: 5–8	Philippus descendens (Pent. v)	XCI	
14–17	Cum audissent apostoli (Pent. iii)	LXXXIX	
26–40	Angelus d. locutus (Pasch. v)	LXXII	
9: 1–22, &c.	Saulus adhuc spirans (Nat. Pauli)	CVII	
10: 34, 42–48	Aperiens Petrus os . . . nobis precipit (Pent. ii)	LXXXVIII	
37–43	Stans Petrus (Pasch. ii)	LXIX	
12: 1–11	Misit Herodes rex (Nat. Petri)	CV	
13: 16, 26–33	Surgens Paulus (Pasch. iii)	LXX	
44–52	Conuenit uniuersa (Pent. vii)	XCIII	
19: 1–8	Cum Apollo esset (Sabb. Pent. h)	LXXXVI	
20: 17–35	Cum venisset Paulus (In aduentu episc. b)	CLXI	

ROM.

1: 1–6	**Paulus seruus I. Christi** (Vig. Nativ.)	I		
3: 19–24	Scimus quoniam quaecunque	*A 42*		
19–26	**Scimus quoniam quaecunque** (Vig. Epiph.)	X		
28–4: 12	Arbitramur iustificari (Oct. Nativ.)		51	
5: 1–5	**Iustificati igitur** (Pent.[3] Mens. Quarti vii. f)	XCVIII*		
6–11	Cum adhuc essemus (Quotid.)	*A 234. We 214*	55, 57	
14–17	Regnauit mors		59	
18–21	Sicut per unius (Apost.[1])	*A 148. We 215*	55, 60	
6: 3–11	**Quicunque baptizati** (Pent.[3])	CVIII. *We 216. A 149*		
12–14	Non regnet peccatum	*AA 34*		
16–18	Nescitis quoniam cui	*AA 23*	57	
19–23	**Humanum dico** (Pent.[8])	CX. *A 150. We 217*		
7: 14–25	Scimus quod lex (Pro seipso)	*AA 54*	64	
22–24	Condelector (Propria)		63	
8: 1–6	Nihil nunc damnationis (Apost.[4])	*A 151*	57	
12–17	**Debitores sumus** (Pent.[9])	CXI. *A 152. We 219*		
18–23	**Existimo enim quod** (Pent.[5])	C. *A 136*	31	
28–39	**Scimus quoniam diligentibus** (Apost. c)	CXLVIII		
35–39	Quis nos separabit (John & Paul)	*A 140*		
10: 10–18	**Corde enim creditur** (Andr. Ap.)	CXXXVIII		

110 *Schedule of the Liturgical Epistles and Lessons*

ROM.			
11: 25–36	Nolo uos ignorare (Pent.²⁵)	*AA 29*	56, 57, 58
33–36	O altitudo (Trinity)		64, 68
12: 1–5	**Obsecro vos** (Theoph.¹)	XII	
6–16	**Habentes donationes** (Theoph.²)	XIV	
16–21	**Nolite esse prudentes** (Theoph.³)	XV	
13: 8–10	**Nemini quicquam debeatis** (Theoph.⁴)	XVI	93
11–14	**Scientes tempus quia** (Adv.⁻⁴)	CXL	
14: 1–6	Infirmum in fide		59
7–12	Nemo nostrum sibi	*AA 30*	
15: 4–13	**Quaecumque scripta** (Adv.⁻³)	CXLI	
14–17	Certus sum		59

I COR.			
1: 4–8	**Gratias ago** (Pent.¹⁹)	CXXIX	31
26–31	Videte vocationem (Epiph.⁵ iv)	*AA 37*	56
3: 8–15	**Unusquisque propriam** (Dedic. Eccl. b)	CLIX	
4: 1–5	**Sic nos existimet** (Adv.⁻²)	CXLII	
9–14	**Spectaculum facti** (Conf. g)	CLI	
5: 7, 8	**Expurgate vetus** (Pascha)	LXVIII	
6: 9–11	Nescitis quoniam iniqui		59, 60
15–20	**Nescitis quoniam corpora** (Spons.)	CLXII	57, 58
7: 1–9	Bonum est homini		58
20–24	Unusquisque in qua (Epiph.³ vi)		59, 60
25–34	De uirginibus (Virgins)		26, 62
32–35	Volo uos sine sollicitudine (Spons.)	*We 188*	32
39–40	**Mulier iuncta est** (Bened. vidue)	CLXIII	
9: 19–22	Cum liber essem		59
24–10: 4	**Nescitis quod hi** (LXX)	XIX	
10: 6–13	**Non simus concupiscentes** (Pent.¹⁰)	CXII. *We 220. AA 24*	
14–17	Fugite ab idolorum		59
11: 20–32	**Conuenientibus ergo uobis** (XL⁶ v)	LXV	
12: 2–11	**Scitis quoniam cum gentes** (Pent.¹¹)	CXIII. *We 221*	
3–11	Notum uobis facio		65
7–11	Unicuique autem		64
13: 1–13	**Si linguis** (L)	XXI	
4–8	Caritas patiens		65
15: 1–10	**Notum uobis facio** (Pent.¹²)	CXV	
12–23	Si Christus praedicatur		57
20–23	Christus resurrexit	*AA 16*	60
39–46	Non omnis caro (Lawr.¹)	*A 162*	55, 57
49	Sicut portauimus		64
51–57	Ecce mysterium		27

II COR.			
1: 3–7	**Benedictus Deus et pater** (Conf. e)	CLI	
3: 4–9	**Fiduciam talem** (Pent.¹³)	CXIX. *A 235*	
18–4: 5	Nos uero omnes (Adv.² vi)		60
4: 5–11	Non praedicamus (Pent.¹³ iv)	*AA 24. We 224*	57
5: 1–11	Scimus quoniam si terrestris (Lawr.²)	*A 163. We 225*	55, 57
6: 1–10	**[H]ortamur uos** (XL¹)	XXVI	
11–7: 1	Os nostrum patet		58

Schedule of the Liturgical Epistles and Lessons 111

II COR.

6: 14–7: 1	Nolite iugum (Lawr.³) (Pent.¹⁵ iv)	*A 164. We 226*		55, 57
8: 12–21	Si uoluntas (Nat. Lucae)	*AA (lh)*		
9: 6–10	**Qui parce seminat** (Lawrence)	CXVII		
10: 17–11: 2	**Qui gloriatur** (Agnis et Agatha)	XVIII		26
11: 19–12: 9	**Libenter enim suffertis** (LX)	XX		
13: 11–13	De cetero, f., gaudete, perfecti			63, 64, 68
13	Gratia dei			65

GAL.

1: 11–24	**Notum uobis facio** (Vig. Pauli)	CVI		
2: 6–10	Deus personam (Oct. P. et P.)	*A 147*		80
3: 6–11	Abraham credidit (Oct. Pent.¹ vi)			59
16–22	Abrahe dicte sunt (Pent.¹⁴)	CXXI. *We 227*		
23–29	Prius autem quam (Oct. Nativ.)			51
4: 1–7	**Quanto tempore heres** (Nat.¹)	IX		
22–5: 1	**Scriptum est enim** (XL⁴)	XLVII		
5: 10–6: 14	**Confido in uobis** (Inuent. S. Crucis)	LXXX		
5: 16–24	**Spiritu ambulate** (Pent.¹⁵)	CXXII. *We 227. A 166*		
25–6: 10	**Si spiritu viuimus** (Pent.¹⁶)	CXXIII. *A 236. We 229*		
6: 8–14	Quae enim seminauerit (Inv. Crucis)			26
11–14	Videte qualibus litteris (Inv. Crucis)			27
14–	Mihi absit gloriari			65

EPH.

1: 3–7	Benedictus Deus (Joh. Evang. a)	VI		
16–21	Non cesso gratias (Pascha Annotina)	*A 101*		57
2: 3–7	Eramus natura			58
4–7	Deus qui diues (Asc.¹)	*A 116*		
11–16	Memores estote			60
19–22	**Iam non estis** (Nat. Apost. a)	CXLVIII		
3: 13–21	**Obsecro vos ne deficiatis** (Pent.¹⁷)	CXXIV. *We 230. AA 26*		
4: 1–6	**Obsecro itaque vos** (Pent.¹⁸)	CXXV. *We 231. A 167*		
7–13	**Unicuique nostrum** (Nat. Apost. b)	CXLVIII		54
17–20	Dico igitur et testificor			59
17–24	Hoc igitur dico			60
23–28	**Renouamini spiritu** (Pent.²⁰)	CXXXI. *A 183, 237. We 232*		
5: 1–9	**Estote imitatores** (XL³)	XL		
10–14	Probate quid sit			59
15–21	**Videte itaque** (Pent.²¹)	CXXXII. *A 184*		
6: 10–17	**De cetero confortamini** (Pent.²²)	CXXXIII. *A 185. We 234*		

PHIL.

1: 6–11	**Confidimus in d.** (Pent.²³)	CXXXIV. *A 238. We 235*		
29–2: 5	Vobis datum est			81
2: 1–5	Si qua consolatio			59
5–11	**Hoc sentite** (XL⁶)	LXI		
8–11	Christus factus est			65
3: 1	Gaudete in d. (Oct. Nativ.)			51

Schedule of the Liturgical Epistles and Lessons

PHIL.

3: 17–4: 3	**Imitatores mei** (Pent.[24])	CXXXV. A 187. We 236	
4: 1	Itaque fratres mei		81
4–7	**Gaudete in d.** (Adv.[-1])	CXLVI	

COL.

1: 3–11	Gratias agere debemus		58
9–11	**Non cessamus** (Pent.[25])	CXXXVI. A 188. We 237	
12–18	Gratias agentes deo	AA 25. We 238	56, 57
21–23	Cum essetis aliquando		59
25–28	**Audistis dispensationem** (Oct. Nativ.)	VIII. We 27	60
26–29	Mysterium quod		69
2: 4–7	Dico uobis ut nemo		59
8–13	Ne quis uos decipiat (Quotid.)	A 239. We 239	51, 57, 69
3: 1–4	**Si consurrexistis** (Sabb. Sanct.)	LXVII	
5–11	Mortificate ergo	AA 17. We 240	55, 57, 58
9–17	Expoliate vos		83
12–17	Induite vos	We 241	34, 52, 55, 58, 64, 68
17–24	Omne quodcunque facitis	AA 19	47, 57
4: 2–6	Orationi instate		58

I THESS.

1: 2–6	Gratias agimus		57
2: 1–8	Ipsi scitis introitum		59
9–13	Memores enim	We 242	56
9–20	Praedicauimus euangelium		81
17–20	Nos autem desolati		58
3: 9–13	Quam gratiarum		59
4: 1–7	**Rogamus vos** (XL[2])	XXXIII	
9–12 & 5: 28	De caritate (Epiph.[5] vi)	AA 45	58
13–18	**Nolumus autem vos ignorare** (Mort. b)	CLXXV	
5: 1–5	De temporibus		59
5–11	Omnes uos filii lucis (Oct. Pasch.[4] iv)	AA 12	56
14–23	**Rogamus vos, corripite** (XL[1] vii. f)	XXXII	

II THESS.

1: 3–10	**Gratias agere debemus** (Conf. h: Nativ.[-5] iv)	CLI. AA 50	
2: 1–8	**Rogamus uos** (Adv.[-2] vii. f)	CXLV	
8–14	Dico . . . reuelabitur		59
13, 14	Nos debemus		52
15–3: 5	State et tenete (Quotid.)	A 240. We 243	57
3: 6–13	Denuntiamus uobis (Pent.[21] iv)	AA 27. We 244	57
13–16	Nolite deficere		58

I TIM.

1: 3–14	Sicut rogaui te	We 245	
5–12	Finis praecepti (Pent.[23] iv)	AA 28	57
15–17	Fidelis sermo, et omni . . . quia (Theoph.[2])	A 16	27, 52
2: 1–7	**Obsecro vos primum** (Aduent. iud.: Lit. maior)	CLXIX. A 113, 225. We 246	54
8–15	Volo ergo viros (Pent.[6] iv. Lit. maior 2)		54

Schedule of the Liturgical Epistles and Lessons

I TIM.

3: 1–7 Titus 2: 10	Fidelis sermo, Si quis (Ordinat. episc. b)	CLVII	
8–13	Diaconos constitue pudicos (Ordinat. diac.)	CLV	
4: 7–10	Exerce teipsum	AA 47	
9–16	Fidelis sermo, et omni . . . in hoc		58
5: 17–21	Presbyteri qui		59
6: 7–14	Nihil intulimus		57, 64
17–21	Divitibus		59

II TIM.

1: 8–13	Noli erubescere (Epiph.[4])	A 20	52, 57
2: 4–10	Nemo militans (Mr.)	A 229	63
8–10; 3: 10–12	Memor esto (Conf. f)	CLI	
2: 19–21	Nouit d. qui sunt eius	AA 46	
22–3: 7	Iuuenilia desideria (In aduentu episc. c)	CLXI	
22–3: 15	Iuuenilia desideria	We 249	
3: 16, 17	Omnis scriptura		72
4: 1–8	Testificor coram Deo (Vig. Sac.)	CXLIX	
17, 18	Dominus mihi adstitit (Quotid.)	A 241	26, 62

TITUS

1: 1–9	Paulus seruus dei (Ordinat. presb.)	CLVI	
7–9 i Tim. 2: 3	Oportet episcopum (Ordinat. Episc. a)	CLVII	
2: 1–10	Loquere quae		59
10	See i Tim. 3: 1–7		
11–15	Apparuit gratia saluatoris (Nativ.)	II	
3: 4–7	Apparuit benignitas (Nativ.)	III	

HEB.

1: 1–12	Multifarie multisque modis (Nativ.)	IV	
13–2: 3 or 4	Ad quem autem angelorum	We 250	62, 64
14–2: 4	Nonne omnes sunt		72
2: 9–3: 1	Videmus I. propter (Asc.[1] vi)	AA 15	56
3: 1–6	Considerate apostolum (Epiph.[3])	A 17. We 29	29, 51, 56, 59
12–14	Videte ne forte	AA 49	59
4: 11–16	Festinemus ingredi	We 252	56, 64
12–16	Viuus enim est dei sermo	AA 32	
5: 1–6	Omnis pontifex (Nat. Pape. c)	CLVIII	
7: 23–27	Plures facti sunt (Nat. Sac. b)	CL	
9: 2–12	Tabernaculum factum est (Pent.[18] Mens. Sept. vii. f)	CXXVIII	
11–15	Christus adsistens (XL[5])	LIV	
10: 19–31	Habentes itaque fiduciam	AA 40	59
32–38	Rememoramini (Plur. Mart. d)	CLIII	
35–39	Nolite amittere (Nativ.[-1] b)	A 209	61
11: 33–39	Sancti per fidem (Sebastian) (Plur. Mart. e)	XVII, CLIII	
36–39	Sancti ludibria (Decoll. Joh. Bapt.)	A 161	
12: 3–9	Recogitate		55

Schedule of the Liturgical Epistles and Lessons

	HEB.			
12:	11–14	Omnis disciplina	AA 48	
	28–13: 8	Habemus gratiam (Pent.⁷ iv)	AA 20	47, 57
13:	9–16	**Doctrinis uariis** (Nat. Sac. c)	CL	
	17–21	Obedite praepositis (Oct. Pasch.¹ iv) (Felix)	AA 9. We 255	56, 58
	20, 21	Deus pacis (Quotid.)	A 242	

	IAC.			
1:	2–12	Omne gaudium		81
	17–21	**Omne datum** (Oct. Pasch.³)	LXXIX	
	22–27	**Estote factores** (Oct. Pasch.⁴)	LXXXI	
2:	1–9	Nolite in personarum		59
	10–13	Quicumque totam legem	AA 33	
	14–17	Quid proderit si		59
3:	14–18	Si zelum amarum	AA 43	59
4:	7–10	Subditi estote	AA 38	59
	17–5: 7	Scienti bonum		59, 60
5:	7–10	Patientes estote (Nativ.⁻⁴ iv)	AA 51	59
	13–16	**Tristatur aliquis** (Pro infirmo)	CLXXIV	
	16–20	**Confitemini alterutrum** (Laetania)	LXXXII	

	I PET.			
1:	1–7	Petrus apostolus (Cath. Petri)		26, 70, 80
	3–7	**Benedictus Deus et pater** (Plur. Sanct. c)	CLII	
	13–16	Succincti lumbos	AA 31	47
	18–25	Scientes quod non (Oct. Pasch.² iv)	AA 10	56
2:	1–10	**Deponentes omnem** (Pasch. vii) (Cath. Petri)	LXXIV	26
	11–19	**Obsecro tanquam** (Oct. Pasch.²)	LXXVII	
	21–25	**Christus passus est** (Oct. Pasch.¹)	LXXVI	
3:	8–15	**Omnes unanimes** (Pent.⁶)	CIII. AA 21. We 102	54
	18–22	**Christus semel** (Pasch. vi)	LXXIII	
4:	1–11	**Christo igitur passo** (Nat. plur. Sanct. d)	CLII	
	7–11	**Estote prudentes** (Asc.¹)	LXXXV. A 137. AA 14	
	12–14	Nolite peregrinari		59
5:	6–11	**Humiliamini sub potente** (Pent.⁴)	XCIX. AA 36	54

	II PET.			
1:	1–	Simon Petrus . . . et Iudas		69
	10–14	Satagite ut per bona		58
	15–19	Dabo autem operam		69
3:	8–14	Hoc non lateat	AA 41	47

	I IOAN.			
1:	4–9	Haec scribo vobis ut gaudeatis	AA 35	47
2:	1–8	Haec scribo vobis ut non (Oct. Pasch.³ iv)	AA 11	56
3:	2–9	Nunc filii dei sumus	AA 39	49
	13–18	**Nolite mirari** (Pent.³)	XCVI	47
	21–24	Si cor non reprehenderit	AA 44	47
4:	16–21	**Deus caritas est** (Pent.²)	XCV. A 138	
5:	1–4	Omnis qui credit		59

Schedule of the Liturgical Epistles and Lessons 115

I IOAN.				
5: 4–10	**Omne quod natum** (Dom. Oct. Pasch.)	LXXV		
18–20	Scimus quia omnis			59
IUDAS				
1: 5–13	Commonere uos			59
APOC.				
1: 1–5	**Significauit Deus** (Nat. Angeli Michahelis)	CXXX		
13–18	Ego Iohannes vidi septem candelabra			69
4: 1–9	**Vidi ostium apertum** (Oct. Pent.¹) (Evang.)	XCIV. *A 160*		
11	Dignus es			72
5: 6–12	Et ecce ego I. vidi in medio throni (Vig. Omnium SS.)	*A 189*		
6: 9–11	Vidi sub altare (Mauricii)			26
7: 2–12	Et ecce . . . Ego I. vidi alterum (Omn. SS.)	*A 190*		27
9–12	Vidi . . . Ecce turba magna (Nat. Sanct.) (Pent.¹)	*A 156. We 114*		
13–17	Respondit unus (Marcellin. et P.)	*A 127. We 115*		
12: 7–12	Factum est praelium (Michael b)	*A 182*		
14: 1–5	**Vidi supra montem** (Sanct. Innoc.)	VII		
13–14	Audiui vocem de caelo dicentem (Mort.)			27, 63
19: 9, 10	Scribe, Beati qui ad coenam			63, 65
20: 1	Ego Iohannes vidi			69
21: 2–5	**Vidi ciuitatem** (Dedic. Ecclesiae. a)	CLIX		
9–27	**Venit angelus et locutus** (Dedic. oratorii)	CLX		

www.ingramcontent.com/pod-product-compliance
Lightning Source LLC
Chambersburg PA
CBHW070109100426
42743CB00012B/2701